Mighty Smallmouth

Mighty Smallmouth

Catching Big Bass on Small Water

By Adam Merrifield

Adam Merrifield, ©2023. All Rights Reserved.

Published 2023.

ISBN#: 978-1-7388687-0-4 (paperback)
ISBN# 978-1-7388687-1-1 (e-book)

Follow the author on Instagram: @seydoggy.fishing

For my wife, who sees the back of me on the way out
the door, more than she sees the rest of me.

For my daughters, who accept that I will never stop
asking them to go fishing with me.

For my son and fishing buddy for life,
thank you for sharing my passion,
and for the many hours on the water.

Table of Contents

Introduction 1
Getting Started 9
    How to Use This Book 9
    Respecting Our Quarry 10
    Water Access 10
    Stewards of the Land and Water 12
    Keeping Safe 13
    Rod and Reel 14
    Fishing Line 15
    A Basic Presentation 20
The Smallmouth Bass 25
Seasons, Time and Behavior 35
    Spring 37
    Summer 38
    Fall 42
    Summary 47
Fishable Features 51
    Understanding Rivers 52
    Meanders, Bends and Pools 54
    Plunge Pools 58
    Current Seams and Eddies 62
    Hard Structure 65
    Soft Structure and Transitions 67
    Overhangs, Undercuts, Shade, and Exposure 69
    Summary 71
Finding Active Bass 79
    Find the Forage 80
    Follow the Birds 83
    Life Cycle 86
    Weather Conditions 88
    Moon Phase 90
    Summary 91
Lures & Presentations 93

Tubes	95
Skirted Jigs	97
Hair Jigs	99
Swimbait & Grubs	101
Crankbaits	102
Jerkbaits	104
Spinnerbait	106
Topwater	108
Summary	112
A Practical Approach	113
Adapting to Change over Time	113
Finding Spots On Satellite Maps	117
Overlooked Community Holes	120
New Sructure, Changing Habitat	124
Oasis in the Desert	127
Worth the Wade	130
Keep an Open Mind	135
The Textbook Play	139
Summary	143
The Final Chapter	145
Acknowledgments	149

Introduction

My love of smallmouth bass started before I knew them by name. As a small boy, my childhood friends and I would wade around Laurel Creek in our hometown of Waterloo. We knew creek chub, catfish and bass, and that was the extent of our knowledge. Catfish repulsed us, certain that they were poisonous, creek chub were boring and ugly, but those rare bass that we would hook up with were the prize of our childhood summers.

I grew up a river rat, in a city that is at the heart of the Grand River watershed, the largest watershed in Ontario, Canada. Living in Waterloo Region, I had immediate

Catching Big Bass on Small Water

access to all the Grand River's tributaries. I lived with a creek in my backyard, rivers, ponds and lakes all within biking distance away, and it was never hard to find a neighborhood parent willing to drive friends and me to any community fishing hole we heard about.

As kids, we had no technique, no pattern, and no actual knowledge of how to target the fish we were after. We'd sit on any river bank, any time of day, and just cast and retrieve. That's why the target species, bass, was so elusive, and catches of any species were incidental. My first glimpse of pattern fishing didn't come until my preteen years on a camping trip with my dad.

On a small lake at the north end of the Bruce Peninsula known for Walleye and Smallmouth Bass, my dad, brother and I would head out on the water at first light each morning. My dad would look for specific features of the lake, watching for signs that fish might be there, observing his surroundings, the birds, and ripples in the water.

This was foreign to me. I was not accustomed to fishing on the water, nowhere near the bank. I was staring blankly at flat, featureless, still water, too deep to see the bottom. All I knew were streams and creeks, and the current that I was used to. All I knew was cast-and-retrieve from the river's edge.

Finally, my dad found what he was looking for, bits of bait and debris surfacing from the depths below. My dad told me to drop my lure there. I did. I waited for what seemed an eternity for my spinner to fall in what was likely 15 feet of water. Finally, it touched the bottom of the lake and my dad told me to raise my rod tip... and that's when it hit... wham!

Mighty Smallmouth

The greatest fighting fish of my life was on my line, which was both scary and thrilling at the same time. I was fishing from a wobbly canoe and this fish was pulling us around the lake. With every leap out of the water, I could see just how big the smallie was, and I worried. How will we land this fish without flipping over, and what will it do to me in the confines of this little canoe?

As a boy, fishing aimlessly from the river bank, I'd only ever seen fish that were 10 inches or less. Now I was fighting a smallmouth that was closer to 16 inches, in the middle of a lake, from a canoe. That day I made the correlation that would forever change the course of fishing for me, keying in on the pattern my dad was showing me—time of day, fishable features, and signs of activity.

What I hadn't known then was that my dad was following the shoreline, looking for an underwater point that fish would relate to. Once he'd found it, he followed it shallower, then deeper, in search of signs that fish may be actively feeding. He was in search of bait balls, blowups, or what he eventually found; debris floating up from the depths.

For the next few years as a teenager, my time on the rivers was more deliberate, more focused, and I was catching more smallmouth bass than I was any other species. I could apply my dad's pattern to the river as well. The bass I was catching were still on the small side, as I would have expected back then. I figured that fast moving rivers only held small bass. That is a view I'd carried with me for nearly 30 years.

When I became a father, my angling aspirations took a backseat while I taught my kids the joys of fishing. I wanted to share my childhood obsession with them, making sure my kids had the best chance of success. All of my children grew up fishing the same community pond where with every cast you were as likely to catch catfish, crappie, and sunfish as you were a bass. We'd while away the summer evenings fishing that pond, enjoying the outdoors more than anything.

As my kids got older and were more interested in other activities (or less interested in fishing with dad), I got the itch to get back into fishing, and back to my roots of chasing smallies. The only trouble was that I hadn't fished on a river in 20 years. I had been "kid-fishing" on ponds for decades. I forgot the basics of how to fish more elusive bodies of water; time of day, fishable features, and signs of activity.

As a busy adult, I had to relegate my fishing days to annual fishing trips with old friends. I probably chased bronze backs in this half-hearted manner for the better part of a decade. It was after a particularly frustrating annual outing that I decided I wasn't fooling around anymore. I went out and bought a small tin boat, 9 horsepower motor and spent the summers hitting up local reservoirs in search of more success than I'd been having as of late.

As I got serious about fishing again, I started dabbling in different rods and reels, baits and lures, boats and kayaks, lakes and reservoirs. I bought books, watched YouTube and researched everything I could get my hands on, from outdoor magazine articles to scientific journals. You'll find, as I did, the media is heavily focused on Largemouth Bass in lakes and ponds, in much warmer climes than I was used to.

Mighty Smallmouth

Just as had happened when I was teaching my kids to fish, my online exploration of today's angling content saw me drift away from my first love of river fishing for brown backs. I was becoming an accomplished angler, catching my share of trophy largemouth, and mastering fishing with sonar on bigger bodies of water. However, I was no closer to my goal of mastering rivers again than I was 20 years ago.

That's when I met local angler Cam Scott (aka @SWOntarioFishing) on FishBrain, whose smallmouth exploits were legendary on our local rivers. Cam was catching 16 inch smallies—and better—daily. I had seen bigger fish caught in the annual bass derby, but I'd always thought they were rare. Encouraged by his many successes and his generous sharing of a tip or two, I finally had the drive to make river fishing my focus.

What I quickly learned, combining my childhood experience with my adult skills, patience and all the research I had done, was that not only can small rivers yield an abundance of 16 inch bronzebacks, but I can catch truly giant smallmouth from streams no wider than half my casting distance.

Over the years that followed, river fishing became an obsession. I now target trophy smallmouth bass, 18 inches and greater, bass that would rival those caught on bigger lakes. Many river anglers are lucky to catch a trophy bass over 18 inches in a season, perhaps even a lifetime. However, In the last two years alone, I have caught and released over thirty bronze giants, many on creeks no wider than 20 feet across.

It is often said that pound-for-pound there is no fish

Catching Big Bass on Small Water

that fights harder, and longer than the Smallmouth Bass. There is nothing like the heart-stopping blow up on a top-water lure, or the freight train impact when a tank of a smallie hits your spinnerbait. A quick search on YouTube and you'll find countless hours of great smallmouth action, leaping out of the water, digging hard as they dive for cover, or head shakes hard enough to peel the line off of the spool. It's easy to see what makes these fish such an irresistible target species.

However, a lot of the content you see or read covers smallmouth fishing in clear water, on big lakes. Content creators on YouTube, or in outdoor magazines alike, are often fishing from a $50,000 bass boat, with $5,000 worth of electronic imaging equipment. The same content creators are often reviewing more lures, expensive gear, and complex rigs than many anglers could use in one lifetime.

The average angler can often view smallmouth fishing as out of their league, with too many lure choices, not enough money for boats and premium rods, or limited access to prime waters. Many will give up when they hit their local water with complicated rigs and only catch dinks, or catch nothing at all.

I wanted to write this book to offer the average angler an opportunity to get on trophy catches on small, accessible, local rivers and streams. My goal is to breakdown the habitat, forage, and behavior of river smallmouth, and build a strategy of simplified presentations to help anglers of any means, ability, or budget, to land truly exceptional bass.

This book won't recommend that you buy a lot of gear

and lures. I won't even prescribe a specific rod and reel. These pages will give you a starting place with some basic background on various presentations. From there, your imagination and ingenuity can take you on your own journey of discovery. Expensive gear can certainly add to your experience and enjoyment, but I'm a firm believer that it is the anglers' skills, not the sticker price of the rod, that help you find and catch trophy bass in your local river system.

Whether you're wading through a stream, fishing from shore, or lazily drifting in a kayak, this book will show you how to use fundamentals, not fancy gear, to help you catch bigger fish. Spring, summer or fall, these chapters will help build your confidence in locating and catching trophy smallmouth bass, using nothing more than keen observation, the simplest of gear, and a deep understanding of time of day, interesting features, and signs of activity.

Getting Started

How to Use This Book

I've broken the book down into logical sections that you can consume in any order. I'd encourage you to skim through various chapters as needed, and then get out on the water and try what you've learned. When you're ready, come back to the book and learn more. I've even designed the book to fit in most tackle bags, so you can take a copy with you.

There is a lot being covered in these chapters, and I don't expect anyone to read it and understand it all in a single sitting. Some of the material won't make sense to you until you go out and explore the water for yourself. Some ideas covered in this book, while often applicable across all smallmouth waters, may not apply to your particular stream or river. That's ok because the teachings within these pages should have you discover what makes you a successful smallmouth angler in your area by teaching you to be observant, and aware of your surroundings.

While I've written the chapters in order of importance (to me), if you're just starting out, you may choose to start in any order that you're curious about. If you want to go fishing in the hottest month, during a full moon, and there's weather rolling in over the next few days, you may choose to read Summer, Moon Phase, and Weather Conditions. Or you may choose to only read up on a bait you plan to use in Lures & Presentations.

Respecting Our Quarry

There is much debate about whether it's better to harvest game fish or practice catch and release. Indeed, many states and provinces have strict regulations regarding fishing seasons, harvest limits and slot sizes. My preference is to practice catch and release, and not to keep any fish that I catch unless I've mortally wounded that fish. That's not to say you shouldn't harvest the fish you catch, but be mindful of the regulations, and where regulations don't adequately protect a population, use common sense.

For example, if I were to abide strictly by my local regulations, I could keep five fish per day between the last Saturday in June, and November 30th. That would equal 795 bass in a single season. I could decimate the collective population of smallmouth in a river system for tens of kilometers, if not more. And in fact, I see this done occasionally. I've fished locations where a shore angler, and his bucket, will return day after day until he can catch no more.

The effects of overfishing can take many decades to recover from, so be mindful of what your fishery can support regardless of regulations. If you practice catch and release as often as you can, and only take fish that are 12 to 14 inches, you can help ensure that smallmouths continue to thrive in your river.

Water Access

I am equally at home in, on, or at the side of the water. Every lesson in this book applies whether you are fishing from the river bank, or standing on the casting deck of a boat. For my local river systems, I've fished from shore, waded in the current, drifted on a kayak, and powered my way around in a Jon boat.

How you get on the river is up to you. Just be sure that the local regulations permit you to be there and allow you to be fishing for Smallmouth Bass. In some jurisdictions, water access is a right, while in others it's a privilege. If you have to cross private property to access the water, make sure you get permission.

Typically, the easiest way to access a river or a stream is from a bridge. In most regions, bridges, the land immediately to either side of the bridge and road, and the land underneath the bridge and road the authorities consider a right-of-way and owned by the crown, municipality, or state. Once on the water, common laws that govern navigable water cover accessibility to most waterways. Most countries have adapted navigable waters acts at the federal level. However, there are cases where the crown or state has granted private ownership of both the easement around the bridge and the waterway itself. While it's rare, it is worth being cautious and looking for private property signs.

I've found in areas where there is contention, you'll see clearly marked survey stakes that show the boundary between private property and public lands.

Stewards of the Land and Water

The main reason landowners with property at the river's edge get bothered by anglers, swimmers and other recreational users is because we usually leave a mess. Whether it's youngsters leaving beer cans or anglers leaving styrofoam worm containers, the mess we all leave behind invariably gets swept up in the next high water event and deposited onto the landowners property.

Besides being an eyesore, the garbage we leave behind can be downright harmful to the river and its inhabitants. I have rescued everything from birds to crayfish that I've found tangled in discarded fishing line. On the river bank, I have impaled myself on discarded hooks. I've cleaned up countless pounds of soft plastic lures tossed on the river's edge, and collected many bags of garbage from under bridges and along the river.

I often bring a garbage bag with me to collect any trash I come across that's safe to collect, and when I don't have a bag, I keep a pocket free in my tackle bag to take whatever garbage I find with me.

Not everyone will collect another person's trash, but we should all be willing to leave a place as good as it was when we found it. Take your own refuse home with you. Whether it's water bottles, old line, discarded lures and plastics, be sure to take it with you when you leave.

If everyone was a good steward of the land and water, landowners would be happy to have us back.

Keeping Safe

Every year there are nearly 5,000 fatal drownings in the US and Canada combined. Even if you think you are a strong swimmer, or the water isn't deep enough, a river can change your perspective in an instant. Even if you have no plans of going in the water, you can find yourself at its mercy.

If you plan to fish in the river (i.e. wading), or on the water (i.e. paddling or boating), consider wearing a personal floatation device or PFD. I recently took a tumble while navigating over a slippery rock in only two feet of water and struggled to get back on my feet. With the current and my waders limiting my agility, righting myself was more difficult than I otherwise would have expected.

It's all too easy to make the smallest mistake and have the deceptively forceful flow of the river turn the tables against you. Wear a PFD if you are not familiar with the riverbed, or are not comfortable reading the river currents you're wading in or paddling on. There is enough to be wary of around rushing water without the added distraction of sharp hooks, and fighting fish.

While I'm bad at this myself, it's always a good idea to travel with the essentials, like some basic tools, a pocket knife and a first aid kit. I've cut myself, impaled my flesh with sticks and thorns, or imbedded hooks deep into my digits. A decent pair of pliers or cutters frequently come in handy.

If you're planning to wade in the river, take it slowly, and cautiously. Even if you can see the river bottom, you won't know how dangerous it is until you fall in it.

Rod and Reel

You might think that this topic ought to cover a chapter of its own. Indeed, most books do. In fact, a lot of books will suggest you need a specific rod and reel combinations for just about every application they can conceive of. There is some validity to getting that specific with your equipment, especially if you fish for a living and every fish counts.

For most of us, the rod we have in the closet is good enough. I prefer different rod and reel combinations, but it has more to do with where I am fishing from and the time of year. But if I only had one rod and one reel, all the basics in this book would still apply.

However, if you're new to fishing, and you don't yet have the gear you need, you might have noticed that there is an endless variety of combinations to choose from. Walking into your local Bass Pro Shops can be downright intimidating. If you are looking to buy your first rod and reel combo and are not sure where to start, I am going to make it easy for you; a seven foot, medium power, extra-fast action rod with a 200 to 300 series spinning reel.

While the above isn't the setup I would typically use (I favor baitcasting equipment), it's the setup I would go with if I wasn't 100% sure what I was going to cast. With a medium power rod, you can throw lures with wide-ranging weights. And the extra fast tip will help the uninitiated feel every detail of the river bottom composition.

The equipment I typically use will vary depending on how I access the water, and I will adjust my lures accordingly.

For instance, if I am wading, I want a single rod that can cast lighter lures and heavier lures, respond well to reaction strikes (crankbait, topwater), and give me decent casting ability in tight confines. For me, this is a typical "crankbait" rod, or a medium power, moderate action rod. This allows me to work jerkbaits, crankbaits, and walking baits, while also providing enough control for jigs and tubes. What I give up on sensitivity, I make up for by using a braided line.

However, if I am sitting in a kayak, I know I have less leverage, so I will opt for a medium-heavy power, fast action rod. Properly working a jerkbait with that rod is a little tougher, but that's also true when sitting in a kayak, so I typically won't pack a jerkbait in that case. The stiffer rod also means I can cast a ½ oz spinnerbait comfortably, which is not the case with my lighter, wading setup.

Fishing Line

Line selection can be critical to an angler's setup and every angler will have their preference. However, the industry places entirely too much emphasis on whether the smallmouth bass can see the line. Just like rod and reel selection, that can make or break your chances of placing in the money of a big tournament, but for you and me, practicality is the key.

I won't prescribe what you should and shouldn't use, but I can recommend keeping it simple. If I am fishing with a spinning reel, I use 10 to 20 pound braided line. I find if I go any lower than 10 pound test; I risk fighting wind knots. If I'm using a baitcaster, I spool up with 20 to 30 pound braided line.

In both cases, the test I choose depends on the manufacturer. I've had success with Piscifun Lunker braid, where the line has a smaller diameter for the same relative strength, so I'll typically use 15 pound test on a spinning reel. With Power Pro Super Slick V2, I'll use 10 pound test, because any heavier test is thicker than I want.

The reason I recommend braid over any other backing line is simply because braid lasts. You can keep the same braided line spooled up for many seasons. Braid makes the perfect mainline, or backing line. Whether you choose to fish with a leader, braid makes the perfect choice to tie on other leader materials.

However, a braided line can have its downsides, which are worth noting. Because of braids' limber nature, it's prone to wind knots, especially on a spinning reel. You always have to pay attention to whether your line has knotted itself up with each cast, or has seated itself correctly on the spool when engaging the bail.

With a baitcaster, using braid can be challenging if you use an inferior make. Braid that is too supple, or has a loose weave, or is coarse, can end up binding against itself on the spool, causing endless backlashes. I've experimented with several brands but always come back to a select few. Piscifun Lunker, for the budget conscious, makes a braid that is roughly equivalent to Power Pro (standard). I will use either interchangeably, but will stick to higher tests (thicker diameter) to lessen the chances of binding. But if lighter line is the preference, then I will stick with Power Pro Super Slick V2, which has a superior grade weave and line coating that performs very well on the spool and resists binding.

For years the debate has raged over whether fluorocarbon, leader or mainline results in catching more fish. I've run tests over several fishing seasons and I can tell you with confidence that it makes little difference in my ability to catch trophy brown bass. In fact, I find the drawbacks to using fluorocarbon outweigh many benefits.

Fluorocarbon does not stay fresh for very long and if not kept in a freezer, it will become very brittle. You will learn this the hard way when you go to set the hook and the line breaks. If you retie and the same thing happens on the very next hook set, you know that your fluorocarbon leader material has gone off.

That's not to say I never make use of mono or fluorocarbon leaders from time to time, but it seldom has to do with whether I think the fish can see the line or not. I will use a mono leader if I'm struggling with the action of a topwater lure, or a fluorocarbon leader if I'm looking to attain better bottom contact. Sometimes I'll tie on a leader if I'm on fish that have violent head shakes. The extra forgiveness can sometimes reduce the leverage a large bass needs to rip hooks out.

On days where I have to soak the topwater lure for an extended period to draw a strike, I will tie on a mono leader. Mono floats, so I can leave it on the water's surface without impeding the lure's action when I go to retrieve it. Braid also floats, but due to braid being so limber, current and wind can see that the braid gets wrapped around the lure (and hooks) if I'm not immediately imparting an action to the lure after casting. Mono, being stiffer, will remain rigidly pointing away from the topwater, keeping my hooks from tangling in the line.

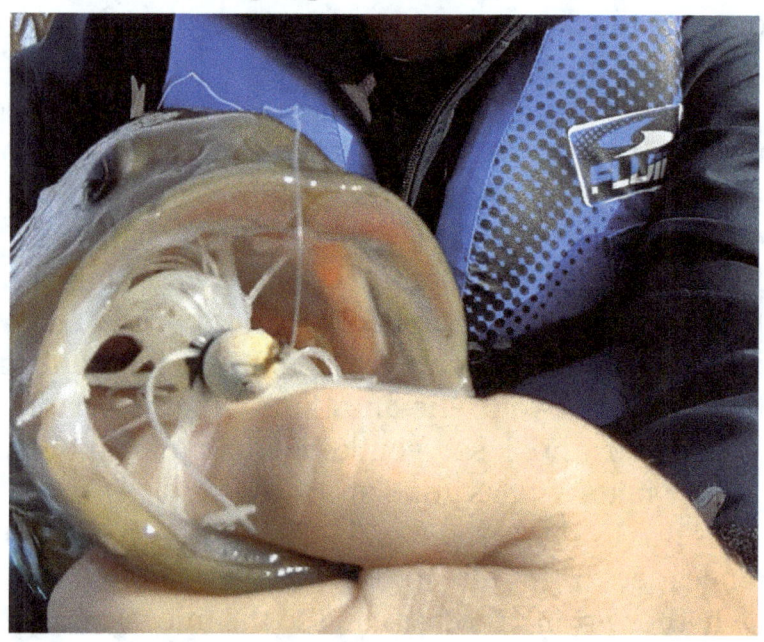

Similarly, when fishing in the middle or the bottom of the water column, if wind and current is creating too much of a bow in my braided line, I may choose to tie in a fluorocarbon leader. Fluorocarbon sinks, which can help keep my lure in the strike zone.

If line visibility doesn't play a factor, why do all the line manufacturers tout reduced, or near invisibility for their various products? Marketing mostly. There are a couple of telltale signs that would reinforce this.

If you've ever looked underwater with a swim mask, goggles or an action camera, you know that even the clearest water has debris in it. The rivers are strewn with filaments and fibers of plant material, man-made debris, bio-waste, silt and so on. Most bass wouldn't pay any attention to the fishing line, as bass wouldn't view it out of the ordinary amongst the other floating debris.

Most cases for using specific line colors or materials are often based on underwater tests where humans assess whether a line is visible. Our eyes and bass eyes are not equal, and our means of vision are nothing alike.

Bass have fewer rod and cone cells, meaning they see fewer colors. They can discern from red and green, but cannot easily tell the difference between blue and black, or white and yellow. For bright light conditions, bass have photopic vision, meaning they have better depth perception and can easily discern from the colors they have available to them. However, during low light conditions, bass have scotopic vision and can see better at night, but lack color acuity.

That's not to say that the bass can't detect the line. Fish can easily detect the least visible of the lines. The lateral line on a bass is a highly sensitive sensory system that allows the smallmouth to detect slight water motions and pressure gradients. One of the finest organs of that system is the neuromast, a series of hair cell sensory structures that spread over the head, body and tail fin. Bass can feel—almost see—the slightest change in the surrounding water. Whether a smallie can "see" the line with its eyes is irrelevant, since it can feel it.

A Basic Presentation

In a later chapter of this book, I will cover lures in greater detail for those who are ready to explore more techniques and presentations. But for now, I want to offer the single most important presentation that will be key to you learning how to fish for smallmouth bass in a river or stream.

One of the key aspects to finding smallmouth bass on a river is to know what sort of features are likely to hold fish. That includes water depth, bottom composition, bottom contours like gravel bars and depressions, and submerged structures like boulders, tree limbs and vegetation.

Short of using electronics, the best way to do that is by exploring the river bed with an appropriate lure presentation that keeps constant contact with the bottom. For that I recommend two options; a tube, and a small skirted jig with a soft plastic trailer.

Few lures have proven to be as productive for bronzebacks as the tube. The tube is candy to a smallie and for good reason. For many decades anglers have relied on the tube to imitate crawfish, gobies, or sculpins, by dragging, scooting or snapping a tube along the river bed between rocks and cover. Tubes are adept at mimicking dying baitfish with a downward spiral of death. They can also be swam through the water column like many minnows, shad or panfish. I can rig them countless ways (I'll cover that in later chapters) for subtle differences in presentation.

Similarly, small skirted jigs, like the many varieties of finesse jigs available on the market (my preference is the Strike King Bitsy Bug), offer many of the same possibilities. From dragging on the bottom, to swimming through the water column, I can make the finesse jig represent just about any forage a hungry smallmouth might be interested in. Paired with many trailer types, the finesse jig can cover all your fishing needs for any outing.

I cover these two presentations first in Getting Started simply because there is no better way to learn about the river. From depth sounding, to gauging current strength, to bottom exploration, these two presentations can tell you more about a section of river in a single cast than trusting your eyesight alone.

The best way to start with each presentation is simple;

cast the lure beyond an area that you feel is promising, then slowly drag the lure back by gently raising the rod tip from 9 o'clock to 11 o'clock. Reel down with slack in your line, back to 10 o'clock and repeat. While you work each lure back towards you, pay attention to the bumps and rolls as your bait knocks around on the bottom and through the current.

At first, you'll struggle to know exactly when a bass has taken the bait, but one thing to remember is that your bait bumps into rocks, not the other way around. When you feel a bump and tension that seems out of place, or notice the line going off in an odd direction, reel down and feel for weight. If the weight pulls back, set the hook. For specifics on the many other ways to fish these presentations, refer to the chapter on Lures & Presentations.

Beyond looking for a bite, you're also looking to understand what the river bottom feels like. When your lure landed, did it tick on rocks, or did it settle in silt? As you drag the lure back towards you, are you scraping across gravel or bouncing over rocks? Have you bumped into a log? Are you getting caught up in some weeds? Did your lure drop off a ledge, or climb a slope? These are details you can glean from these two simple presentations. While it may seem impossible at first, you will gradually get a feel for what your lure is coming across at the bottom of the river.

Using bottom presentations to learn about a section of river is a skill that can take time. Dragging a lure across the bottom can be a frustrating experience for the uninitiated. Don't let snags and hangups discourage you as they tell you a great deal about the river bed, and can also lead to hookups with curious bass waiting to see what your lure does after being freed from the crook of a tree. Often a smallmouth can't help but react when a tube suddenly pops violently out from under a rock. Learning the tricks to freeing up a stuck lure is a big part of river fishing and one of the more important skills to learn early on. It's also an effective tactic to trigger aggressive smallies.

The Smallmouth Bass

Ask me why I'm obsessed with catching smallmouth bass (Micropterus dolomieu) and I am hard pressed to give you a simple answer. A cousin of the largemouth bass (Micropterus salmoides), we often think of the smallmouth as the lesser of the two black basses. From books to magazines, YouTube to professional angling societies, we give largies the lion's share of the attention.

There are plenty of good reasons for this. The largemouth bass is responsible for a $60 billion industry with over 30 million participants in the US alone. The greenbacks are readily available across North America, and tolerate the hottest southern US states and the coldest Canadian lakes. They are easy to target, easy to predict, and always willing participants in a tug of war between man and fish.

The smallmouth bass is considerably more elusive. Their territory is significantly less—sticking mainly to cooler northern climes—and not readily found farther south than northern Alabama. And since their behavior can vary so widely from one population to the next, targeting them with common, consistent patterns can prove difficult.

What makes the smallmouth bass one of the most exciting freshwater sport fish is their sheer determination and grit. They rarely give up the fight, often performing aerial acrobatics, leaping many times their body length out of the water. Hooking up with a brown back is not a guarantee of landing one. Without the right technique, playing the bass out just right, a smallie will keep digging and thrashing until they've pulled those hooks clear out of their jaw. I've fished in smallmouth waters where the population was so aggressive that it was a struggle to land three of every ten hookups.

An aspect of smallie fishing that can be challenging to many anglers is their ability to disappear. You can find a lively stretch of water, and catch them all day long, only to have that area produce no bites on subsequent visits. You may find a time of day that reliably sees the fish frantic to swallow your bait, only to have that bite shut down moments later. Some days you could approach the river with a marching band in tow, and still catch a bag of smallies. Other days, the wind and the rustling of the grass spooks the bass.

There is no better feeling at the end of a harrowing smallmouth fight than lifting an 18 inch specimen, or better, from the flow. Having conquered a most respectable adversary, with heart pounding and knees weak, you inspect your quarry. Its form is like no other; sleek, powerful and built for the river.

When in peak form, they resemble the profile of a football, so thick behind the head and around the middle, they look like they have shoulders. Everything about their fusiform shape lends itself to being a superior swimmer, being able to hold effortlessly in the current. It's also what allows them to fight so hard, making them one of the more powerful fish to tug at the end of a line. Their lifetime spent in the current gives them the stamina to keep the fight going well past the time when their greenback cousins would quit.

Mighty Smallmouth

No two smallies are alike, but all are beautiful to behold. Some are a light gold with few markings, while others can be dark brown or nearly black. Some have the markings of a cheetah right off the African savannah, yet many smallmouth bass will be striped like a bengal tiger from the jungles of India. Unlike the cheetah or tiger, however, a smallmouth bass can change its markings to suit its environment.

Smallies found in lighter colored water, in silted areas of the river might be a lighter shade, with stippled stripes and blotches, while a few bends up the river in a highly vegetated, well-shaded area might find the population of smallmouth to be a deep chocolate brown. If the population downstream were to move to the same vegetated section, they, too, could adopt the darker color in a matter of minutes. In fact, males guarding a spawning bed can often be black, and can change from very light to dark black in less than an hour.

The coloration and powerful build of a smallmouth bass make it a formidable ambush predator. Smallmouth can hold tight to a river bed, blending in perfectly, waiting to strike at its next unsuspecting victim. Smallies are also curious, and abundantly bold, so we can often find them cruising lower in the water column in search of forage. They will readily eat most things that move into their strike zone, which is surprisingly large. They will actively search for hellgrammites (dobsonfly larvae), crayfish, sculpins, darters and gobies on the riverbed, while keeping an eye out for baitfish higher in the water column. Anything that falls to the surface from an overhanging tree is fair game as well.

Seasonally the smallmouth will gorge itself on midges of all varieties, from mayflies, and caddisflies, to dragonflies, and many midges and nymphs. Smallmouth are opportunistic feeders and will take advantage of any source of protein. They seem to be keenly aware of the lifecycle of many winged forages about to hatch or emerge from the water. Many fly fishers take advantage of this by "matching the hatch" with the flies they cast. There are regional hatch charts available for most rivers, helping fly fishers know what to cast at certain times of year.

Generally, in the warmer months, all bass are crepuscular feeders; mostly active at dawn and dusk. You'll often hear anglers refer to the morning bite, or the evening bite. What's interesting about smallmouth bass studied in river systems across North America is that you'll find no two populations to be the same in their daily activity levels. You'll find populations to be crepuscular, while others are active all day.

Indeed, if I break down my statistics across each of my home waters, I get varied results. In one of my favorite rivers I see most bites at 8:00 a.m., 3:00 p.m. and 7:00 p.m., while in another river the greatest activity starts after 11:00 a.m. and goes on until 4:00 p.m. In my experience, you can find smallmouths that will bite any time of day if you know where they are and what presentation is likely to cause a strike.

As a hearty freshwater fish, the smallmouth bass is equally at home in deep glacial lakes as it is in small creeks. From open water fisheries like Lake St. Clair, Lake Ontario, St. Lawrence River, to narrow creek channels cutting through Carolinian forests, as long as the water is cool enough and relatively free of pollutants, the smallmouth will thrive.

There is a lot of emphasis on a smallmouth's preference for clear water, the argument being that they are primarily a sight oriented predator. However, several productive rivers that I fish have low visibility more often than they have clear running water. Don't discount a river or stream because of its turbidity. Many rivers will become muddy or "blown out" after a rainfall and many anglers will avoid fishing during these times. I've found that low visibility does nothing to deter bass from biting.

Using their natural ability to feel the ebb and flow of

the current, smallies position themselves advantageously in current seams, in the pools behind rocks or in the hydraulic cushions ahead of boulders. Many anglers believe bronzebacks need large enough structure to hide behind, but a bass can hold in the currents that are dampened by softball size stones, or a sudden change in the bottom relief (sandbar or scour pool). Even during extreme flooding, a smallmouth needs only to move closer to the river bank to get relief from the relenting flow.

Late one October, after a week of solid rain, I braved kayaking down a river that was flowing at 45m3/s, four times the normal summer flow. What was worse was the 27 km/h winds blowing upstream, making white caps that flowed both upstream and downstream. To my surprise, I landed an 18 and 16 inch smallie burning a small paddle tail swimbait with the raging current. The 18 inch smallie hit so hard and fast that the hook was just past its crushers. Even in the most blown out flows, with less than 1 foot of visibility, smallmouth have no difficulty finding their prey.

There is also a widely held belief, made popular by at least one study released by the Minnesota DNR, that smallmouths migrate great distances, often daily. It's also believed that they migrate upstream in the summer, and migrate downstream in the fall or winter. This idea persists, and while smallmouth can, and often do, migrate, it's not a hard and fast rule. If a population of smallies lives in a section of river with sufficient forage, shallow spawning areas, and deep water pools, that population will never leave that section of river. I know of many such locations.

Mighty Smallmouth

If an area provides for a smallmouth's seasonal needs, a population can spend its entire life in a couple thousand square meters of river. That includes deeper pools for over wintering and hot summer conditions, shallow spawning flats for reproduction, and forage. If a bass migrates can be determined by these aforementioned factors.

Another aspect of smallie physiology that causes basic needs is their response to water temperature. There are key temperature ranges that will trigger certain activity in smallmouth that are worth noting to better understand where they may be. In water temperatures below 40°F, bass are in winter mode. They'll hold in deeper pools, but will still eat occasionally, despite their slow metabolic rate. For water temperatures between 40°F and 50° a smallmouth bass' metabolism will support modest growth.

With temperatures between 50°F and 60°F the smallmouth bass will be on a feeding binge. In the spring, as the temperatures climb, this feeding frenzy will support the coming spawn. All spawning activity takes place at around 60°F. In the fall, the heavy feeding helps bass put on weight to support the winter fast.

Between 60°F and 80°F after the spawn has completed, smallmouth are actively hunting all day. Anything above 85°F becomes difficult for the bass and their activity will be limited to dawn, dusk, and even during the cooler nights.

Now that we know the basic behaviors of the smallmouth bass, it's time to learn how to find them. In the following chapters, we'll unlock the basics around time of day, interesting features that would hold fish, and looking for noticeable activity in your surroundings. You'll find that these three components go hand in hand for your everyday outing. When coupled with other factors such as weather, moon phase and seasons, you'll soon be able to predict when an outing is likely to be exceptional.

Mighty Smallmouth

When in peak form, they resemble the profile of a football.

Catching Big Bass on Small Water

Smallmouths do not need clear water or noisy baits.

Seasons, Time and Behavior

The best time of day to go fishing is the time you have available. There can be more productive times during that day that you could fish, but if you can't be there at that given time, you won't be catching them, anyway. However, having an awareness of what happens at various times of day can help you better cater to what the smallmouths are more likely to respond to.

As a general rule, smallmouth bass are most active at dusk and dawn. Probably these are the times of day when their prey is most vulnerable, cast as silhouettes at the water's surface against a lighter sky, while the watery depths shroud the bronzebacks in darkness at the bottom of the water column. Dawn and dusk are also the times of day when bass are least vulnerable to becoming prey themselves. They are no longer visible to eagles, hawks and herons, allowing them to venture further into the shallows in search of baitfish.

But smallmouths aren't simply responding to a sundial at 5:00 a.m. and deciding it is time to eat. Bass are opportunistic predators and will eat any time the appropriate prey comes into view. And that's exactly what's happening at these times of the day. A lot of their forage is coming out of hiding right when a smallies superior eyesight is allowing them to home in on them.

Apart from their own concern of being prey themselves, smallies have no trouble chasing bait all day, and will do so when and where the conditions are favorable to them. It just so happens their most opportune times, when their forage is active, is at dawn and dusk... during the warmer months.

You can't separate time of day from time of year, and what that means for the length of day. Time of day, and by extension, daylight, is what makes the ecosystem operate. If you look at the cyclical nature of the seasons, March 20th and September 22nd have days and nights of equal length (equinox), yet the fishing in each season is not comparable. Fishing during dawn or dusk in March will have dramatically different results than it will in September.

If you consider what time of day is representing at a particular time of year, the notion that smallmouth bass are "crepuscular" (active at dawn and dusk) holds little meaning because that is only relevant during the warmer months. I'd say that the rule applies between late June and mid-August, and only if there isn't a full moon, weather front, shad spawn, and so on.

Except for extremophiles, most of the life we know on earth depends on the sun. The energy harnessed from the sun's rays is chemically converted to life giving compounds by phytoplankton and bacteria, which are consumed by zooplankton, larvae, midges and nymphs, which are consumed by baitfish, which are consumed by... and so on.

The sun is literally the catalyst of it all, the engine that powers the factory of life. When you have more sun, you have greater energy imparted into the ecosystem. The greater the energy, the greater the activity; within limits. So let's look at how time of day changes the way you fish throughout the course of the day, and how that line of thinking needs to shift over the course of the fishing season.

Spring

March 20th marks the date on the calendar when the period of daylight—having increased gradually in duration since the winter solstice—and the period of nighttime is equal; the spring equinox. In the northern hemisphere, the sun angle will increase with each passing day, making days longer and gradually warming up the earth, air and water.

Activity within nature increases with this increased warmth. Snow melts, and freshets rejuvenate streams and rivers, carrying nutrients into the watershed. These deposits provide the first boost of energy needed to kick start the life cycle of phytoplankton and zooplankton. Everything comes alive with food sources replenishing and waterways warming slowly.

Depending on how early or late spring arrives in your area, you may see signs of life in the shallows by late March or early April. This may happen on sunny, warmer days later in the afternoon as the sun's energy heats the shallower water and the river banks. You may find baitfish and even smallmouths sunning themselves. During these first few weeks of spring, mid afternoon is the most productive time.

As we move from early April to mid-May, the days are getting longer and the factory of life is bringing out the smaller forage. Insects and minnows are emerging and cruise the shallows. A larger window from midday to late afternoon has opened up, and the bass are chasing small forage. Presentations best suited for panfish are also going to attract the attention of smallies. Everything, by this point, has woken up and is hungry.

By mid-May to mid-June, smallmouths are putting on the feedbag to prepare for the spawn. In fact, by early June, many males will already be on beds. The days are getting pretty long by this point, nearing the summer solstice, and the water is warming up quickly by now. Productive times are going to be early to midmorning, through to the evening. Because the bass are bedding, they'll be out all day.

Given that late spring into early summer is critical to the bass' lifecycle, I don't recommend targeting them. Even if local fishing regulations permit it, avoiding spawning smallmouth is the most eco-friendly approach to ensure healthy populations for years to come. With that in mind, however, it shouldn't surprise you at just how aggressive smallmouths are at this time of year. While targeting just about any other fish, smallies will probably be the first fish to take a swipe at your lure.

Spring recap:
- Early spring: mid afternoon
- Mid spring: midday to late afternoon
- Late spring: morning to evening

Summer

The longest day of the year, the summer solstice, occurs on June 21st, and marks the first day of summer. Depending on how far north or south you are, this may also coincide with the approximate time that the spawn has wrapped up. This is also the start of the season where you may notice true crepuscular behavior.

Mighty Smallmouth

In the first few weeks of summer, with the sun at its zenith, the full power of its rays is rapidly warming the air and water, and shoreline shadows are increasingly scarce. The spawn is nearly complete and the smallies are resuming their normal lives. This can mean many things to different populations in different rivers.

For some populations on bigger rivers, with ample forage, this can mean nothing much has changed. They'll resume their daily routines, sit comfortably in their deeper pools, cruise for an easy meal in a run or glide. Life will go on.

With other smallmouth populations on smaller rivers, or where forage is scarce, individual specimens may migrate great distances in order to eke out a spot on the river of their own. Because of this behavior, it can sometimes be difficult to locate bass for the earliest part of summer.

Whether the bass have moved or stayed put, the morning and evening bites will be more prevalent in your fishing, while during midday, shady spots and deeper pools will still produce. For all day fishing, look for river sections in deep-cut valleys, or flowing up against steep bluff walls. The added opportunities for shade will keep the smallies cruising.

Early July to mid-August are the dog days of summer. These can be truly difficult weeks for fishing, physically and mentally. There is certainly a correlation between morning and evening bites. Deeper pools and shade still play a role in midday action, but dawn and dusk are when the bronzebacks will feel most lively. If you're one to consider night fishing, this is the time of year for it, especially with a full moon in a cloudless sky.

These summer doldrums come down to heat. Depending on how cool your river runs, you may find the bite doesn't shut down quite the same. But if your section of river is above 79°F, you will find the smallmouth less willing to take part in a protracted battle with rod and reel. At dawn, smallmouth will be apt to cruise the river banks in search of food, but as the sun heats the day, they will retire to deep pools or seek shade. They may also set up just downstream of riffles where the water is often cooler. As the sun sets behind the trees and the shadows lengthen, the bronze back will begin foraging again.

If the water temperature stays within the favorable limits of the bass, you may still find them difficult to find and catch, because of the high angle of the sun in midsummer. Smallies will seek cover while the sun shines directly on the water, depending on water clarity. I fish clear rivers at high noon, where the bass will hide under stumps, and inside mink or otter holes to evade the ever-present bald eagle that roams up and down the river. While in other rivers with low visibility, the smallmouth are happy to hang out at the bottom of a deep pool in the bright sun, knowing the eagle can't see or reach them.

A smallmouth's willingness to bite during the heat of the day can be dramatically improved if other factors are at play, like weather fronts, moon phase, forage activity and water conditions. Case in point, two days after a full moon, on the hottest day in July, I struggled all morning to get a bite. By mid afternoon the sun, high in the cloudless sky, was baking everything it touched. I didn't think there was much hope of anything biting and I considered packing it in.

Mighty Smallmouth

That's when I noticed some baitfish activity skipping around the water, trying to evade some unseen predator. Given the time of year, and the full moon still in effect, this was likely a shad spawn, and where there is a shoal of shad, there are predators. I threw a spinnerbait through the heart of the activity and reeled at a fairly fast rate... WHACK! My spinnerbait was hammered by a 19.5 inch tank of a deep brown bronze back.

With my spinnerbait in knots, and not wanting to miss out on the feeding frenzy, I quickly lobbed out a Berkley Choppo... SMASH! A dark smallie with deep bars exploded on the Choppo. The next two casts landed a pair of 16 inch smallies. This non-stop action went on like this for an hour, and as quickly as this bite turned on, like the flick of a switch, it was over. On the hottest day, full sun, blue sky, midafternoon, I had one of the most productive hours of fishing in my life.

As late summer rolls around and the days get noticeably shorter, the fishing really starts to pick up, and baitfish is the name of the game. More comfortable water temps and the shorter days trigger the smallmouth bass to get serious about bulking up for winter. If your section of river has tributaries and inlets, you may find the smallies pushing (or following) bait fish into the backs of these channels.

As the nights get colder, the water temperature will gradually drop, potentially slowing down the dawn and dusk bites, while morning and evenings will still play a big factor. During midday, the smallmouth will still make use of shade and deeper pools, but these hides become less prevalent and the desire to feed drives the bass on as

the summer begins to cool towards fall.
Summer recap:
- Early summer: morning, evening, pools and shade
- Dog days of summer: dawn and dusk
- Late summer: morning, evening, pools and shade

Fall

The autumnal equinox, September 21st—the second day in the year where night and day are of equal length—marks a magical transition in the smallmouth's behavior. Winter is fast approaching and animals all across the northern hemisphere are making preparations for the long period of famine ahead.

There is no better season for smallmouth fishing than fall. If I could only fish for one month of the year, it would be October; it's fast, exciting and the bass are so aggressive. The fishing changes daily as cold nights and cooler days, mixed with cool nights and warm days, and water temperatures fluctuate. The weather changes so fast that you can generally break it down into two main parts; before and after mid-October.

Before mid-October, the water is dropping to a smallmouth's ideal temperature. Knowing that winter is around the corner, the smallies become frantic, and put on the fall feedbag. An 18 inch bass that would have weighed 2.5 to 3 lbs in the summer suddenly weighs 4 lbs. It's not uncommon to catch 16 inch smallmouths that weigh over 3 pounds.

By this point in the season, you can reliably find the bronzebacks holding near their wintering holes. Look for sections of the river where the water is at least four feet deep and can hold a healthy population. Bass will rarely winter alone. You'll find the bass here overnight, but they venture out into the nearby shallows during the day, in search of warmth and food.

Expect to have some tough days mixed with some exceptional days. In a recent fall season, I was landing 18 inch smallies, and bigger, each day. There were plenty of 17 and 16 inch catches as well. But one afternoon when I had only a couple hours to fish (including paddle time), I got onto a group of true fall giants. From 2:20 p.m. to 3:20 p.m. I landed three tanks, all over 18 inches. I knew I was likely in for some nonstop action if I could have stayed, but sadly (and painfully) I had to go before I could find out.

It's tough to call one time of day better than the other during this two to three-week period at the start of fall. Generally, from sunup to sundown is fair game, but it really depends on the weather over the last couple of days. If it's been cold for a few days, stick to midafternoon. If it's been warm for sequential days, then as soon as the sun hits the water, you should find the fishing to be productive.

After mid-October is when the fishing can get tough, but so rewarding. The water temperatures are falling fast and the opportunity for bass to sun themselves in the shallows becomes fewer. Baitfish are slowing down or die off, and the water temperature on the coldest days has the metabolism of smallmouth at a near standstill. On the coldest, most overcast days where the water temperature has caught up to the air temperature, your luck will be in short supply.

But these mid-fall days still have a few warm surprises in store. From day to day, mid-fall can see wild temperature swings, often bringing a "second summer" after frost-covered mornings have become the norm. These are the days when you can catch true trophy bass.

It was early November in 2020, after weeks of frigid days, hats, coats and gloves, when the temperature suddenly swung upwards, bringing on a "second summer". It was T-shirt weather, and time to fish for giant smallmouth. The water had equalized with the air temperature weeks before, so I knew the water would still be icy cold. I knew exactly where to find them on the first day of this unseasonably warm spell; sunning themselves in the shallows next to a deep pool.

I made my way to one of my favorite spots on the Grand River, in the heart of Waterloo Region. It was midafternoon, warm and sunny, and I knew the sun's rays would have had the greatest impact by then. This section of river warms on sunny days because of a large, shallow flat caused by a bend in the river. There are certain times when I know the smallmouth will hold up here, and on a day like today I knew I'd find a few taking advantage of the sun's added energy.

My first cast was made at a 45° angle from the bank, down current. At this section, the pool transitions into a glide, and there is a slight back-eddy just about casting distance away. I knew the current would bring my bait (3.5 inch green pumpkin tube, ¼ oz ball head jig) back in towards me, and right in front of where a healthy population will often hold up behind a sandbar in 2 to 3 feet of water.

Mighty Smallmouth

I let my tube roll in the current a little before I started a slow, gentle drag towards me. Slowly raising my rod from 9 o'clock to 11 o'clock, reeling up the slack and repeating. I could feel my tube slowly climbing the sandbar I was so familiar with. As I crested the sandbar, I braced for the possibility of a bite. I could feel my bait become ever so slightly lighter as gravity aided its descent down the gentle slope of the sandy ridge.

That's when I felt the undeniable tap of a smallmouth picking up my tube. I hesitated… a smallmouth will often shake a bait, spit it out and pick it back up, or at least work the bait around as it repositions the lure. Often a smallmouth will start to move away with your bait, especially if it feels challenged by others in the pod. But neither of these things happened.

Carefully, I picked up some line to see if I could detect some weight on my lure, a sure sign of a bite—and there it was. I pulled a little, the fish on the other end leaned back, and like lightning… THWUNK! I set the hook with a sweeping upward stroke of the rod. The weight on the other end of my line was undeniable. This was going to be a solid bronze back.

The smallie headed out into the main current, peeling the line off my spool as she went. She tried to swing back downstream, which gave me the opportunity to guide her back my way into a slower flow. The resistance this fish was giving was steady but sluggish, a continuous weight that flexed my rod, but without repeated head shakes and thrashing. I got her up to the surface within ten feet of my position. That's when I saw how big she truly was. Easily a trophy bass with potential to be so much more.

She dug in, but with only eighteen inches of water to work with, she could only swim a wide, sweeping arc. She leapt from the water and dove again, this time heading for the deeper current just beyond the sandbar. We played this game for a few more minutes as I played her closer and closer to the bank. Now only in six inches of water, I waded out to lift this truly magnificent deep bronze beauty from the river.

This fall-fed, "second summer" treasure of a smallmouth bass measured 20 1/4 inches and weighed 5 1/4 pounds. She was bigger than I ever dreamed possible in this central section of the Grand. This was my personal best river-caught smallmouth bass, and she was a fit, healthy, and immaculate specimen who showed no obvious signs of having been caught before.

After a quick release, I cast back to the same spot. Same slow drag... THUMP! I reeled in a second trophy smallmouth at 18 inches, followed by a third cast... WHAP! A third 18 inch smallmouth. Three casts and three trophy bronze backs in under 20 minutes. I landed the first trophy smallmouth at 2:44 p.m. and landed the third at 3:02 p.m. With wobbly knees and a pounding heart, I thought it was best to leave the rest of this family of sunning smallmouth alone and headed home.

The November "second summer" stayed with us for another six or seven days, allowing me to catch a 19.5 inch, and three more 18 inch smallmouth trophy bass in three more outings before the cold set back in and shut the bite down. Arguably, this was my best week of fishing that I'd ever had on a river, as far as size is concerned. This was a week that truly helped me unlock river fishing.

Fall is always bittersweet. It marks the end of the smallmouth fishing season for me, but is always the most exciting and productive time to fish. For me, the rest of the year is practice as I get prepared for fall fishing.
Fall recap:
- Before mid-October: mid afternoon, or sun hits water
- After mid-October: follow the heat of the sun

Summary

In this chapter, we learned that the time of day, the time of year, and the length of day are all factors that drive the ecological engine of life. Increasing daylight in the spring warms water and triggers life to become more active. Midsummer heat drives bass and forage to seek cooler water and limits activity to dawn and dusk. Reacting to shorter fall days, smallmouths will aggressively start to feed to prepare for winter, capitalizing on second summers in the waning days of fall.

Now that you understand how seasons drive a smallmouth's behavior, you need to know where to find them on the river. In the next chapter, we'll look at how to break down a river so that you can identify which sections of your local river are likely to be productive, high percentage areas.

I avoid spring bass fishing, even if the regulations allow it.

Mighty Smallmouth

Blue skies, high sun, blazing hot... most anglers would hide.

Catching Big Bass on Small Water

My personal best river smallmouth.

Fishable Features

Knowing when to fish is only part of the equation. Knowing where to fish is arguably more important, since even a fish who's not keen on eating can often be coerced into biting if you put a lure in front of them. But you have to know where they are first.

Many anglers might read this chapter and think I'm talking about "structure", so why am I calling it "features"? There is a distinction between the two; structures are the objects that hold fish nearby, such as dock pilings, tree stumps and rock piles, while features are geographic or erosional formations, riverine or stream characteristics, and structures that collectively make for sensible locations that would hold bass.

When river fishing, I find looking at features is more useful than simply considering what structures might hold fish. A recent laydown (structure) in the river won't hold fish if it's beached in 12 inches of water with fast flowing current around it. But over time, the current flowing past that tree will erode the substrate around the fallen tree and create a backwater pool, or a lateral protrusion pool. The structure alone isn't enough, but through erosional forces over many years, this structure and the pools associated with it have become a fish holding feature.

So let's break down what to look for in a river system and what features are likely to hold fish, and which are not.

Understanding Rivers

River systems have common features that repeat over their course, which maintain slope and stability. Any healthy stream that is free of artificial impoundment will follow either a low slope pattern of riffle-pool sequence, or a high slope step-pool sequence. All the rivers I fish locally fall into the low slope category.

The low slope riffle-pool sequence is vital to a stable river system that can maximize the distribution of water and sediment using as little energy as possible, moving as slowly as possible. The riffles are key to this energy distribution. Riffles are shallower, steeper sections of the river composed of larger cobble and boulders. The flow is greater at riffles and typically more turbulent, aiding in oxygenation and sediment distribution.

Pools are found after riffles, and are considerably deeper, calmer sections of the river that flow significantly slower than the riffles they follow. During low flows, pools collect sediment and rubble discharged by the riffles. However, during high flow, through velocity reversal and shear stress reversal, pools will relinquish their sediment and rubble and deposit them onto the next riffle. Through this continual exchange, rivers maintain their meandering stability over thousands of years.

Depending on how expanded or compressed the riffle-pool sequence is, runs and glides can be found at the head and tail of a pool, respectively. A run will immediately follow a riffle, with a deeper, less turbulent, and slower flow rate of the riffle. The glide, immediately after the pool, will have a shallower, faster flow rate than the pool, but will share its characteristic flat surface.

Impoundments that permanently block the river's natural course, such as dams, weirs and barrages, alter this natural relationship between riffles and pools for many miles upstream. Sediment collects over time for many miles upstream of the impoundment and is never redistributed downstream. This can often leave impounded river waters less ideal as a smallmouth habitat.

So which river features are likely to hold smallmouth? It entirely depends on the flow rate and size of your particular section of river, but as a general rule smallmouths are rarely found immediately in the riffle. In my experience, smallies are distributed in the runs, pools and glides. Where and when will depend on several factors like river flow, bottom composition and the additional features (geomorphology and structure) found within each.

During low flows, I find more fish in the run and near the front of the pools. At times of high flow, I focus my attention more towards the back of the pools and in the glides. If the pools are vast—hundreds to thousands of meters squared—I look for riverbed composition that will either hold forage, or provide ample current disruption. A weed line, a patch of softball sized rocks, or a transition from rocks to gravel or sand will often hold groups of smallmouth. In runs and glides, I focus on structures that provide current breaks, like boulders and laydowns.

Meanders, Bends and Pools

When left to nature, over many hundreds or thousands of years, a river will naturally wind its way, or meander, through the landscape. As water flows down a channel and hits a bend, the balance between pressure forces and centrifugal forces causes a helicoidal flow, which is important to know when fishing river bends.

The helicoidal flow, if you were to imagine it, is the churning of the river—at the surface, from the inside bend towards the outside bend, curving under down to the riverbed, then from the outside bend back across the riverbed to the inside bend, and back again. So the river corkscrews through the bend while still flowing downstream. It's this helicoidal flow that causes the outside bank to erode and get deeper, as the inside bank gets shallower when sediment that can no longer be carried by the flow is deposited there.

Learning to see and understand this complex flow of water in a river bend will help you better locate fish that may live in them. Knowing the water flow will move across the bottom will allow you to master the right presentation, ensuring that your bottom bait is pulled towards the bass in the direction they're facing. Your ability to detect the subtle current changes as this flow interacts with obstacles on the riverbed will be key to getting your bait to where the fish may be holding.

As you will find, river flow rate can dramatically change or enhance characteristics of the current. A high flow rate can reveal boils and eddies caused by unseen riverbed obstructions that otherwise would go unnoticed. A previously undetected current seam can reveal a change in the riverbed elevation, a sandbar or a transition of bottom composition. These are all areas to make a note of when low flows make it harder to see these disturbances.

As briefly mentioned in Understanding Rivers, changes in flow rate can also determine where the smallmouth will position themselves in the bend or pool. High flows can often find smallies moving to the downstream end of the pool, even pushing back into the glide. High flows can also find the bass closer to the banks, especially the inside bend, where flow rate is less significant. In low flows, however, smallmouths can push to the upstream end of the pool and into the run.

On some rivers, the deepest pools may also serve as the smallmouth's overwintering location. If the conditions are right, a group of smallmouth may live out their entire lives there. Not that I fish for smallmouth bass in the winter, but finding a pool that can serve this purpose means that I know where to find them all season without worrying about migration patterns.

The scale of a meander, bend, or pool will vary on the size and flow rate of the river you are fishing. A tiny river I frequent, a deep pool may be less than a meter deep and the entire length of the bend may be only tens of meters long. Another, larger river that I frequent has pools that are over two meters deep and the bends are hundreds of meters or even kilometers long.

Meanders, bends and pools are likely the highest percentage location to catch smallmouth, but locating them in deeper water can be challenging. Exploring the pool riverbed with a bottom presentation is key to finding the structure that a bass will relate to. Look for a series of rocks, a transition from sand to gravel, a weed line, a boulder, a submerged tree, a sandbar or depression. Make a mental map of these areas. They will be your spot-on-a-spot areas.

On a relatively slow, low-gradient river that I fish often, the meanders are many. The river snakes through the countryside changing direction regularly. It's not uncommon to wade around bend after bend in a few short kilometers. Some bends are shallow with long sloping beaches on the inside with only a narrow channel of deeper water, while other bends are seemingly bottomless, hiding fallen trees and other structures in their depths.

On a hot August afternoon I visited a new stretch of river I had yet to explore. After wading around two bends, I finally came upon one that showed promise. The water darkened quickly, just upstream from the glide at the tail end of this pool. A few meters up from there were signs of a current break that was certainly a submerged tree.

From close to the inside bank, I cast my topwater lure towards the outside bend, behind the obstruction. I had expected a strike, but to no avail. I then cast ahead of the submerged obstacle, and with a few strokes of the rod... THWOP!

I had engaged with an aggressive 3.25 pound brute measuring 19.5 inches. This girl put up a heck of a fight as she tried to take me into the rocks that I could just make out between me and the outside bend. After a minute or two I could safely coerce the smallie to the inside bank and land her.

Breaking down a larger pool or bend can be daunting, but looking for features that bass can relate to can help you focus on key, high percentage areas.

Plunge Pools

Plunge pools are deep, erosional cavities in the river bed formed when the turbulence from water flowing over harder rocks erodes softer riverbed substrate behind them. A plunge pool will form more frequently at the tail end of a riffle but can also occur anywhere the conditions are met. Over time, the water flow will erode the riverbed, wearing a deeper depression. As more material is washed away, the farther the drop and the greater the erosional forces. Over many thousands of years, plunge pools could form waterfalls.

On a narrow, relatively slow river I fish there are vast stretches of slack water that are deep enough to be considered typical pools of a riffle-pool sequence, but I rarely find trophy smallmouth living here. Instead, because of the compressed nature of the riffle-pool sequence, I more often find the biggest smallmouth living solitary lives in

Mighty Smallmouth

the smallest of plunge pools immediately after the riffles.

It was early morning on July 22. I was wading downstream from a bridge I had briefly explored once before. Having only coaxed a single smallmouth to strike at top-water in the slack water near the bridge, I continued downstream. I came upon a double riffle-pool sequence compressed to less than 60 meters of river. Knowing these extra turbulent flows would erode the riverbed, I was fairly positive the pools would be exceedingly deep despite their small size.

In the first pool I tossed in a weedless jig with a plastic trailer, simply to gauge the depth. My jig dropped about eight feet. I was standing in less than two feet of water and my lure was only six feet in front of me. This pool dropped deep and did so quickly.

Soon after my lure hit bottom, before I could even pick up the slack in my line, I had a small 15 inch smallmouth take my bait and give me a little tussle. I knew this pool was big enough to hold more fish, but I wanted to see what the next pool behind me held.

The next riffle immediately downstream had a similarly turbulent flow, but was accompanied by a sharp bend that created a current seam on one side, and an eddy on the other. I opted to throw a top-water over the current seam into the slack water and reel carefully back upstream. There was an angry, almost desperate explosion at the surface near the back of the current seam. I paused, then continued to reel... another blow-up! I paused again, briefly, before starting to reel again. My heart was pounding, desperate for another strike... SPLASH! She connected hard and was making for the heaviest flow into the deepest pool.

The fight was exhilarating, especially after two false starts (you rarely get a second chance at a top-water, let alone a third), and this girl did not disappoint. She thrashed about, leaping from the water, shaking my lure violently. Her anger only got her further tangled in my hooks, ensuring that she had no escape. When the fight was over, I added another 18 inch beauty to my growing list of trophy catch-and-release bass that year.

A few weeks later, and a twenty-minute drive downstream on the same river, I was wading beyond a familiar section in search of new features that might hold a giant or two. I came to an old train bridge that over the last century had constricted the river flow to two tight channels on either side of the central bridge pier, each producing a shallow, turbulent riffle. Immediately after one riffle I noted the convergence of two turbulent currents that looked very much like the hydraulic jump you see at low head dams. The area was no bigger than a bathtub, but I suspected there was more depth to that spot than the surrounding water would otherwise show.

I was standing in only a couple of inches of water. The water around the current feature wasn't much deeper, but the current itself looked to be holding secrets. On a hunch, I threw a top-water bait clear over the current in question and quickly reeled upstream. The instant I hit that hydraulic jump in the flow, FFTHWASH!

I was certain the smallmouth had missed, so I didn't set the hook right away, but then I felt her weight and knew I had a tank of a bronze back on my line. The fight was short since I was only a few feet from this hidden plunge pool and was only in inches of water myself. What I raised from the shallows was the skinniest 19 inch trophy I'd caught that season.

My final example of a plunge pool catch came from the same river just days later. Considerably farther upstream this time, I waded the length of a long, slow pool. It was a dry summer, and the flows were uncharacteristically low for this time of year. The deepest section of the pool I was wading through was only knee deep. I suspected many of the smallmouth had moved in search of deeper, cooler water. The many unproductive kilometers I had waded seemed to support this hypothesis.

I approached a downstream facing v-shaped riffle, where I spotted a cutaway on the left side bank, just after the turbulent water. The surface was unusually calm and looked to have a bit of a swirl in it, making this little spot, only six feet around, look suspiciously deeper than it should be. Once again I was standing in less than a foot of water, but I've learned in this river that plunge pools can hide in the most unassuming water.

I cast a top-water lure across the pool to the river bank behind it and started to reel back towards me. Upon reaching the middle of this tiny pool, my bait was blown clear out of the water when a giant smallmouth annihilated my lure. The bronze back immediately made for the middle of the river, headed downstream towards safety. I wrestled her back upstream, and once I had settled her down, I claimed a 19.5 inch smallmouth for the books, only my second of three 19.5 inch trophies of that season.

Learning to read the signs of plunge pools can reveal deceptively deep water, an ideal ambush point for a giant river smallmouth.

Current Seams and Eddies

A current seam is the delineation where two areas of water that are traveling at different speeds meet. Seams can be caused by an obstruction in the current, like a fallen tree, a wing dam, a boulder, or simply a change in the riverbed like a drop off, sandbar or weed line.

Not everyone can read water well enough to know a current seam when they see it. It's not an easy thing to understand when all you see is flat water, or rough water, and it may all look the same to the untrained eye. Some current seams are easier to see, some require surface foam or floating debris to see well. If you train yourself to see them, current seams are a key feature to explore.

Smallmouth bass can detect the subtleties of current through their lateral lines and the series of neuromasts

Mighty Smallmouth

along their head, body and tail. This allows them to sit at the edge of the slower water or in an eddy and wait for baitfish to swim by in the faster flow. Swimming a lure downstream right at the edge of the seam can often yield those bass waiting for an easy meal.

Understanding what is creating the current seam is as important as finding it. You don't need to know the exact nature of the obstruction or transition, but you need to understand whether the fish would be set up behind an obstruction or in front of it, on top of a transition, or on the leeward side of it. This will tell you where to start and finish your presentation.

A shoal or wing dam, for instance, will create a long seam that will delineate the river flow from an area of slack water or an eddy. You can find fish all along this seam, but may find them concentrated towards the obstruction as there is likely to be a lateral protrusion pool immediately after. I will use this knowledge to throw my lure upstream and work it downstream past the obstruction. Where possible, I will try to swim the lure into the slack water and over any expected pools.

A large boulder, on the other hand, will have a seam on each side of the boulder, an eddy, and potentially a pocket pool behind it. Depending on the size of the boulder, you can find several fish stacked up on the backside. When that's the case, you can expect the biggest of the smallmouth will be in that pool taking prime position.

I will usually throw well ahead of the boulder and see if I can't pick off a smallie riding the hydraulic cushion ahead of the boulder. I'll work that lure down either side of the boulder and occasionally try to catch the eddy to bring my bait back in behind the rock.

I more often have luck with boulders that are positioned in runs rather than glides. That may have more to do with my ability to position myself better on a run. In glides I find smallmouth anywhere, not necessarily just behind boulders. With runs being faster and more turbulent, the boulders are likely helpful to the smallies, more so than they'd be in the calmer water of the glide.

One often overlooked, yet obvious current seam, is the confluence of two rivers. This provides not only a seam between two bodies of water traveling at different speeds, but also offers the possibility of divergent water temperatures, or a differential between water clarity between the two water sources.

It's this difference in water clarity that can often provide the most advantageous fishing opportunity. Smallmouth bass are known to congregate at a river confluence, but when a turbid river and clear river mix, the effect is more pronounced. Sometimes, I've seen smallies lined up in the clear water waiting for unsuspecting bait to swim clear of the muddy water. In a more surprising twist, I've experienced it the other way around where the bass hide in the muddy water and wait for bait to enter their strike zone.

Hard Structure

Regardless of the river feature I'm fishing, I always look for the structure that sits within that makes it an area interesting to smallmouth. In runs, pools and glides, in meanders and bends, looking for the structure gives the smallmouth an opportunity to hide, rest, or go deeper is always an advantage over barren, open water. Whether the structure is strategic or simply something the bass can relate to, any variation in the riverbed is a feature that potentially holds smallmouth.

Hard foreign structures such as fallen trees (laydowns) can offer a variety of advantages for smallies. Depending on the seasonal flows, that structure may only be temporary, washed away in spring flood or fall high flows. Temporary laydowns can add a new opportunity for smallmouth to hold in areas not previously known to hold them. Always make note of where last year's laydowns have come to rest this year.

Larger, or more permanent laydowns that hold fast to

the riverbed offer an opportunity for smallmouth to return year after year (or stay all year long). A laydown as a fixed position will offer significant current breaks that smallmouth will naturally take advantage of. Over many years, that same current break creates lateral protrusion pools, or backwater pools which provide additional current breaks and deeper water for smallies to live in.

In my experience, if an entire tree has made it into the river, its root ball will usually face upstream with trunk and limbs directing downstream. This makes for typical flow patterns that can be easily exploited. I often fish the front of the root ball thoroughly as there is a hydraulic cushion that smallmouth will take advantage of. At the base of the root ball, I will explore the pool underneath created by years of erosion. Then I will work along the

underside of the trunk, and the far side of the trunk and around the tree limbs as I work my way downstream. Weedless or snagless presentations will help the inexperienced, but knowing how to work any lure through carefully, or over wood, will even allow the experienced angler to use open hooks.

Another favorite feature within a feature that I have great success with is sprawling rock deposits. Pools are often dominated by silt and sediment, but I've found that some pools have just the right flow and bottom composition, that the riverbed is almost entirely made up of softball size rocks. When this occurs, I know the entire riverbed can hold smallmouth bass.

When I find such an area, I know just about any presentation will work, but I typically locate the active bass with paddle tail swimbaits, a crank bait, or spinnerbait worked downstream. Once I've located the area where they're holding on that day, I will work the bottom with a tube or finesse jig to get the bigger, more wary bronze backs. If I'm familiar with the rock fields already, I'll go straight to the bottom bait. I just love popping a tube over top of a rock to have a smallmouth smack it before it hits bottom again.

Soft Structure and Transitions

Soft cover like weeds, grass, reeds and other vegetation are often thought of as largemouth bass hiding places. Most vegetation doesn't take hold in faster current, or the sediment deposition required for plant growth is frequently washed away, but in key river features that will also support weed growth, you can find smallmouth bass as well.

Finding a vegetated area is a good sign that you've found slower water, or even a pool. Vegetation provides hiding opportunities for bait fish, therefore provisioning forage for smallmouth bass. I find the higher percentage spots on a weeded area are the edges. I will often swim a lure downstream just over the outside edge, or I will work a bottom presentation just beyond the weeds. Occasionally, pulling a lure through the weed bed itself will catch a smallmouth hiding within.

The edge of a weed line represents another important feature that smallmouth will often relate to; transitions. As the riverbed gives way from one composition to another, this can serve as a transition. An example would be sand to coarse gravel or rocks, a steep drop, rock slab or shale, to rubble; transitions seem to offer a visual cue for smallmouth bass to relate to. Using a bottom bait to explore and understand the riverbed of a pool can help you locate these transitions and use them to your advantage.

One such transition that I know of goes from an array of medium size rocks which abruptly transitions to sand or silt. I've caught so many trophy bass on that transition that you think they'd have learned by now.

Overhangs, Undercuts, Shade, and Exposure

Sometimes steep or straight banks of an outside river bend will offer another favorite hide for smallmouth bass, especially on hot sunny days; overhangs and undercuts. Both occur when the river flow erodes the rock and soil from the riverbed at, or below, the waterline, while the earth above the waterline remains stable.

Undercuts will offer significant shelter from sun and keep a smallmouth hidden from birds of prey, but they may also offer the same break in current that you'd expect from hard structure. The added surface area and complex helicoidal flow created in an undercut may allow a smallmouth to exert far less energy to hold inside one.

Cover that is good for smallmouth is also good for a plethora of other organisms as well, attracting many of the bass' main forage types. From crustaceans, to invertebrates, and baitfish, all will use an overhang for shelter. A smallie can simply wait for a meal to come to it.

Overhangs don't strictly come as river banks. In fact, overhanging trees can offer many of the same comforts to a smallie as an overhanging bank. Many anglers will shudder at the thought of casting under an overhanging tree for fear of getting tangled there, but the rewards can be worth the risk. I've caught many trophy smallmouth hiding under the shade of a weeping willow dangling just inches off the water.

When all other forms of cover are absent from the smallmouth's chosen haunt, the bass will simply seek the shadiest part of the river (see Season, Time and Behavior for seasonal exceptions). This can easily be determined from a satellite view of the stretch of river you wish to fish. In the northern hemisphere, the shadiest side will be a southernmost bank. In the morning, an east bank will be the shadiest, and in the evening, the west bank will be in shadow.

Trees lining the river will only enhance this effect, and a narrow river cutting through untouched Carolinian forest may benefit from shade for most of the day. Of course, in the cooler seasons when predatory birds are less threatening, smallies may choose the warmer, sun-kissed banks to live on. In which case, the opposite is true to all the above.

Summary

Learning to fish rivers, understanding how to read the water and knowing how to locate high percentage areas that hold smallmouth bass can be a daunting process. Understanding rivers and their common features, knowing where and how pools occur, and learning how to use structures within various river features to your advantage can help make your task of locating smallies easier.

So far we've learned about the smallmouth bass, how seasons and time of day affect their behavior, and where to find them in a river. What happens when you have the season and time of day just right, and you found a pool with the perfect laydown, but no matter what you try, you just can't seem to find a bass willing to bite? In the next chapter, we'll cover how an understanding of your environment and surroundings will help you sense when a bite is on or not.

Catching Big Bass on Small Water

Targeted casts to identifiable features pays off.

Mighty Smallmouth

The third strike was the charm.

A life in strong current has worn out this skinny 19-incher.

Mighty Smallmouth

Plunge pools can hide giants in otherwise shallow rivers.

Catching Big Bass on Small Water

A 19.25-inch trophy bass hiding behind a boulder in a fast run.

Mighty Smallmouth

Transition from medium rocks to sand or silt holds some big girls.

Finding Active Bass

Whether we are aware of it, all animals, including us, are affected by subtle changes in the weather, air pressure, moon phases and many other environmental conditions that we may not be consciously aware of. Sometimes you can feel a storm coming on, or some days you feel more lively than others. We've all joked about how crazy moods are attributed to a full moon, but there is more truth to these phenomena than not.

Have you ever driven down a country road and been surprised by the active wildlife? Groundhogs out in the open, and vultures riding the thermoclines. Red-tailed hawks perched on the hydro wires, crows squabbling over roadside carrion, or maybe an unexpected deer or moose sighting in broad daylight. Days when the trees are full of birdsong, and the grasses buzz with crickets and cicadas.

You may have also noted the days where the countryside seems devoid of life. No birds, no squirrels, and the fields and woods are eerily quiet. I can recall one evening, while staying in a remote location in northern Ontario, I was enjoying the steady din of night insects and nesting birds all competing to be heard. I knew vaguely that a breeze was picking up speed, but it wasn't until all the insect and bird songs fell deathly silent that I knew something was about to happen.

Within minutes, the skies opened up and the most torrential downpour of the season swept across the land and water. Winds whipped and lightning struck and sheets of rain were deposited on any exposed surface. By this point I was safe and dry in my cottage, but only hours before the fishing was unbelievably productive as the smallmouth prepared for the coming storm. No one knows exactly why this behavior occurs, but it's a well-known phenomenon.

Smallmouth, like the rest of the living organisms, are in tune with the environmental changes around them. They follow cycles; they follow forage, they're a slave to the seasons and are living fully exposed to whatever mother nature throws at them. We've already discussed the obvious changes because of seasons and day length, but in this chapter, I want to cover some of the less obvious indicators that can lead you to smallies that are willing to bite.

Find the Forage

Mighty Smallmouth

I wish I could remember the study or article I read this in (I think Gord Pyzer has something to do with it), but essentially they tagged some smallmouth to see how far they'd travel in search of food. Many smallmouths will travel great distances in search of, or following, their prey. However, it turns out that some specimens didn't move at all. If there was a decent forage base where they were, there was no reason to move. This really drives home the point that regardless of all other conditions listed in this book so far, if the food isn't there, the bass won't be either.

We've all caught a smallmouth that looks like it's missed a few meals, and certainly an advantageous ambush position in the river will sometimes trump an abundance of food, but it's a pretty safe bet that if food never crosses that smallies path, she is going to move on or die. On many lakes this makes chasing smallmouth so tough, they can travel many kilometers per day following their forage. They can go north, east, west and south. They can go shallow, run deep, tuck into bays or suspend in open water. Finding them from day to day on a lake is a bit of a 3D guessing game. However, on a river, they can go upstream (to a point) or downstream (to a point), so even if they migrate in search of food, your efforts at finding them are somewhat linear.

The forage base for smallmouth bass in a river system can be broad and varied, from the many types of invertebrates and crustaceans to many baitfish. Rivers have the advantage that food is bound to wash by, eventually. However, smallmouth will set up in areas that are more likely to house multiple food sources. Knowing the patterns and behavior of the bait will help you follow them.

Crayfish and other invertebrates such as leeches and hellgrammites will prefer a riverbed with large rocks to hide in, but they also prefer a substrate that they can burrow in like clay. A combination of rocks with a clay foundation is ideal. Any section of river that is suitable for crayfish will also be suitable for many invertebrates, especially hellgrammites. Find a section of the river with adequate opportunity for a crayfish or hellgrammites to hide and you will find smallmouth.

Similarly darters, sculpins, sticklebacks and goby—all bottom dwelling baitfish—will prefer rocky bottoms with ample hiding opportunities, but will also be found on gravel beds and occasionally on sandy bottoms that transition between rocky or gravel bed areas. Each species generally prefers faster, cleaner water and will spend most of their life cycle within a short range of river. For faster moving water that holds darters, sculpins, sticklebacks and gobies, look for current breaks that would be advantageous to a smallmouth bass. Spotting these bottom oriented fish is easiest when wading through the water as many will flee as they avoid coming under foot.

Small bait fish such as shiners, minnows, dace, and chub (we'll collectively refer to them as minnows) will live in many environments depending on the specific species. The ones that smallmouths care most about are the ones that live on gravelly or rocky river beds in swift, clean currents. Following these minnows can be a lot of fun as smallmouth will corral schools or shoals of them against a bank and then pick them off as they stray from the group. As water temperatures drop in the fall minnows will start to struggle and die off. Smallies will take advantage of the struggling minnows and aggressively prey on them. Minnows can often be spotted near the surface in shallows or along banks.

Occasionally on some rivers I run into large shoals of gizzard shad. This is usually in late fall to early winter as the shad are seeking warmer water. Shad are often found in deeper, more vegetated, turbid waters so they can be tough to spot, but when they are being chased by prey, they will repeatedly leap from the water to escape. If you see this occur and can make them out to be shad, it's a safe bet that tying on a shad presentation will yield results.

Follow the Birds

The best indicator that I am close to active smallmouth bass is the presence of birds. I'm talking about seabirds like herons, egrets, loons, cormorants, and seagulls, and birds of prey like terns, kingfishers, osprey and bald eagles. When there is more activity from the air and above the water, there is more activity below it.

As solitary hunters, egrets and herons will eke out a living picking off enough bait fish to sustain them from just about any location on the water. But when I find several of them crowding a section of river, I know that a smorgasbord of bait is on its way through. The smallmouth will have taken notice as well. Position yourself downstream of the herons, as they will often be near a riffle or choke point to pick off the baitfish in the shallows, while the smallmouth bass will be in the rear, driving the baitfish upstream or up against the riverbank.

I rarely come across loons or cormorants on my small, swift local rivers, but I know from experience on larger river systems and lakes that they are a good indicator of baitfish being present. And where there are baitfish, there are smallmouths. On the other hand, I will find seagulls on my local rivers, but only when certain migrations occur, or if there is spawn activity in a certain baitfish. Either way, when I see loons or seagulls, I know I'll find smallmouth nearby.

I usually only find terns, osprey, and eagles in open areas of the river or bigger sections of river because of their need for airspace to see their prey, dive for it, recover and repeat. However, when I spot these birds in the trees or in the air, I take it as a good sign that the fishing is good enough for these birds to call this section of river home.

Mighty Smallmouth

This is especially true with osprey and eagles, as the fish they need to support their diets, and rearing young, are larger specimens, like smallmouths, trout, pike and carp.

Kingfishers are an interesting little bird that I've come to rely on to lead me in the right direction. When I find one of these hand sized birds flitting about in the trees along the river bank, it's a good sign that baitfish are abundant. But what I've also come to learn is that the more active they are, the more active the baitfish are, and the better my fishing is. In particular, if there is a weather system moving in, I have to fight to keep these little guys from attacking my bait. It's on these outings that I will have success in finding a good sized smallmouth.

A word of caution about following the birds. If you spend enough time in the same locations, or the areas you fish are frequented by many other anglers, the birds will become accustomed to anglers and what angling ultimately means. Occasionally, I've had herons within a few meters of me attack my lure as they watched me work a topwater lure across the river. In one case I briefly hooked a heron, and was worried I'd have to attempt a release on an angry heron with a sword of a beak.

Likewise, a flock of seagulls can be relentless if you're trying to work a topwater lure within sight of them. There are times I've had to move to a less productive location simply to avoid the onslaught from seagulls.

And of course, there is the danger of having your catch stolen by an eagle or osprey. This has happened to me twice, and fortunately, both were at safe distances, but there are well documented occasions where large birds of prey will swoop down and snatch a fish right out of an angler's hand. The potential for real harm coming to both angler and bird is high in such cases.

Life Cycle

JasperWV, CC BY-SA 4.0, via Wikimedia Commons

Smallmouth bass will spawn in late spring to early summer or when the water temperature is between 55 to 70 degrees Fahrenheit. Males smallmouth will build and guard small, round nests, typically constructed in the rocky shallows with some relief from the current.

The arrival of a female spurs a ritual that will cause the female to deposit her eggs for the male to fertilize. The male will remain and protect the eggs, fiercely warding off predators such as gobies, crayfish and rock bass. During the entire spawn, the male won't eat, so once the eggs are

Mighty Smallmouth

hatched, the male will stick around to guard the fry for another week or two before venturing off to feed.

During the spawn, the male is highly vulnerable, fending off anything that comes close to its nest, even a lure. For this reason, I am strongly opposed to fishing for bass on beds. In fact, in my region, the fishing regulations prohibit it.

However, the spawning cycle sets up two very predictable feeding periods where bass will be fairly aggressive; immediately before the spawn, and immediately after. Once the water temperature reaches 50° and smallmouth move towards their preferred spawning grounds, they will also look to bulk up for their long fast. Similarly, after the spawn has completed, males will look to replenish themselves after many weeks without sustenance.

If your local fishing regulations allow it, immediately before and after the spawn can be two productive times to find active smallmouth bass, but be careful to avoid vulnerable males on their spawning beds.

Weather Conditions

No single factor has a greater impact on my fishing success than the weather, specifically the weather fronts that are moving in or out. Temperature fluctuations have very little immediate impact since the water will slowly raise or lower in temperature over several days. However, the weather fronts that bring in those temperature fluctuations, warm and cold fronts, trigger different feeding behaviors that can either turn the fishing on or off. Weather fronts also bring many phenomena worth using to your advantage, such as high winds, rain, or clear, sunny skies.

Weather fronts can be broken down into two main groups; cold fronts and warm fronts. Cold fronts are a dense mass of colder air pushing up against warmer, less dense air. As the cold, dry air moves in, it pushes the warm, moist air higher, which will aid in the formation of clouds. Cold fronts are accompanied by higher winds and a drop in barometric pressure. Winds, overcast, pressure drop, potential rain, all combine to turn on the bite.

Warm fronts, as you would expect, are the opposite with warm, less dense air displacing colder, dryer air. However, the effects can be similar, with high winds, rain, overcast or fog. However, instead of settling into overcast conditions, a warm front settles out into clear, warm skies with high barometric pressure. Again, the rapid change in conditions often triggers the fishing to become more productive.

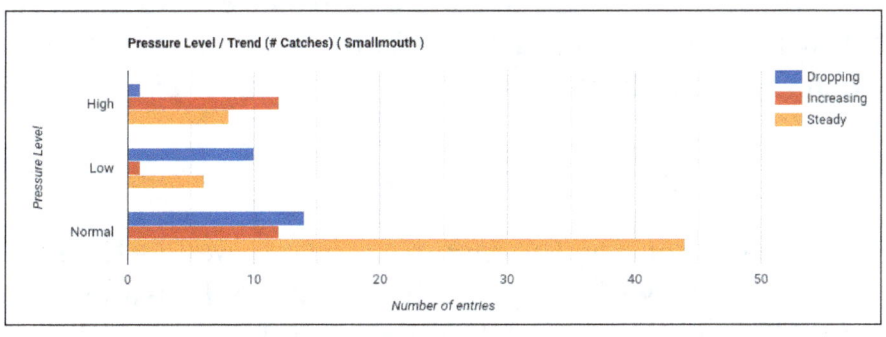

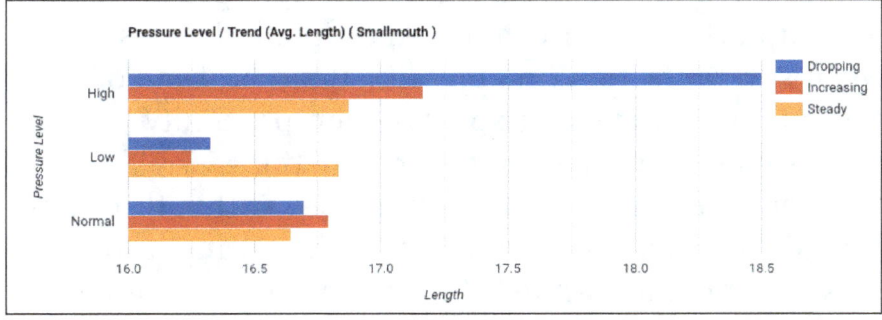

So what about in between, when air masses are stable and air pressure is somewhat normal and steady? The weather under normal conditions is stable, with winds that follow the sun's movement, air pressure is stable, the sky can be overcast or clear, but generally constant. This is when fishing can be most difficult, and I'll pay more attention to seasonal behaviors, fishable features, and finding their forage than I do the weather.

While a cold front is moving in, I catch more smallmouth bass while the barometric pressure is dropping. However, I catch the biggest trophy smallmouth once the low pressure has stabilized. During a warm front I will catch the most smallmouth while the pressure is climbing, but the biggest smallies as the pressure starts to drop from those highs. With normal air pressure, I catch more fish while the air pressure is steady, but the biggest bass when the pressure increases.

Moon Phase

I've been tracking the moon phases, as well as the solunar calendar, with every catch since 2019. I wish by this point I'd see some correlation that I could prove with the data, unfortunately I cannot. Anecdotally I can say that when several factors line up—like weather, time of year, water temperature, bait spawn—then proximity to a full or new moon seems to count for something.

Some of my best fishing days happen within three days of a full or new moon... sometimes. I have caught some giants late at night... while fishing by the light of a full moon (not something I typically do). I've also had terrible days of fishing on both full and new moons. Taken as a factor on its own, it's difficult to conclude that the moon phase has any real effect without considering the many other conditions that drive bass behavior. But it's something many anglers just feel matters, myself included.

Gord Pyzer has explored the phenomenon of how a full moon can affect the feeding patterns and growth of ecosystems. Pyzer suggests that clear skies during a full moon can provide added light, creating additional feeding opportunities for the ecosystem, which promotes the growth and molting periods of crayfish. Freshly molted crayfish are easier and more energy-efficient to consume than those with hard shells, and smallmouth bass know this.

To test this theory, I set up an aquarium containing crayfish with constant light and dark cycles, consistent water temperatures, and regular feeding. I found my crayfish molted within three days of a full moon several times per year, regardless of the amount of light or food available.

The full moon may influence the behavior and patterns of crayfish, and perhaps the rest of the ecosystem. Anglers and hunters have long relied on the solunar schedule, which considers the phases of the moon, to determine the best time to fish or hunt. While I have had some great experiences during a full moon, my sample size is too small to make any definitive conclusions. I will continue to collect data to identify clear trends over time and try to understand other factors that contribute to successful outings. Until then, I will make a note of the moon phase and solunar theory before heading out to fish.

Summary

Tuning in to nature and the activity level of your surroundings will help you find active smallmouth bass. Are the songbirds singing? Are the crickets chirping? Are there baitfish swimming lazily about or are they breaching the water's surface to escape predators? Are the river banks lined with herons, and the skies full of gulls? Are there shoals of spawning baitfish? Is there a storm rolling in? Being in tune with nature and your surroundings will be a factor in your ability to find trophy smallmouth.

Lures & Presentations

As the old saying goes, lures are designed to catch anglers, not fish. If you spend any time reading outdoor magazines and websites, or watching fishing related YouTube and social media, you'd quickly conclude that you need many hundreds of dollars' worth of lures in your tackle box. Every author and content creator will extol the virtues of throwing a specific lure and color combination for a specific time of day, season, cloud cover, water temperature, water clarity... By this logic, the list of lures and colors you'd take to the river would require a pack mule.

The truth is, catching smallmouth bass is not complicated and the lures that I used can be broken down into these basic categories; it crawls, it swims, it floats, it struggles. I don't like to limit my terminology to "reaction baits", "finesse baits", etc, because I may use a "finesse bait" in a reaction style presentation, or I may slow a "reaction bait" down so slow that it becomes finesse. Instead, I like to categorize my lures by the presentations they are capable of.

For example, a skirted jig with a crayfish trailer can be crawled along the bottom like a crayfish or crustacean. It can be swam through the water column like a baitfish. Or you can start and stop the retrieve, allowing the jig to fall down to the bottom, like a baitfish that is struggling to survive.

Similarly, a jerkbait can be slashed, twitched, jerked and paused, similar to the behavior of a dying or struggling minnow. Or a steady retrieve will emulate a baitfish swimming in the water column. If your jerkbait is the floating kind, you can use a slow retrieve and work the bait just below the surface, creating a tantalizing wake that bass love to key in on.

For these reasons, I can pack very light when I hit the river. I typically pack a topwater bait (it floats), a spinnerbait (it swims), a jerkbait (it struggles), a skirted jig (it crawls), some ball head jigs, and a handful of soft plastic baits. I will change this lineup slightly at different times of the year, but mostly, I'll cover the four categories in a single plano box.

My simplicity also applies to color selections. White, green pumpkin, black/blue, and gray are my go-to colors, with orange, blue or red being accents. I try to match the forage as best I can, so I will use green pumpkin for crawling presentations with blue or red accents, white underbellies for swimming presentations with blue or orange accents, black for invertebrates like hellgrammites and leeches.

Let's go over some of my favorite lures and presentations that have landed me some of the biggest bass to ever come out of small rivers.

Tubes

Presentation: *it crawls, it swims, it struggles*

The tube is my all-time favorite lure when fishing for trophy smallmouth bass on a small river system. As explained in the Getting Started chapter, the bottom presentation is ideal for discovering what the bottom is made of and what lies between you and the lure in front of you.

While there are many ways to rig a tube, my preferred method is to keep it simple and rig it "open", using a 3.5 inch green pumpkin tube (any brand will do), with a 1/4 oz ball head jig and 2/0 hook, inserted internally. This is your standard tube set up. You can drag this presentation on the bottom. You can hop it, snap it or crack it (crackin' a tube), stroke it, and even swim a tube. With the tube rigged open, each time the tube falls back to the riverbed, it will spiral, making it appear like a dying baitfish.

Another popular way to use a tube is Texas rigged. With a bullet weight and an EWG hook, you can use the popular setup like you would any other texas rigged soft plastic. This is great for punching through weeds, and pulling through brush piles, but since neither of these are high percentage areas for smallmouth, I rarely rig my tubes texas style.

In a similar vein, rigging a tube with an EWG hook, but without the bullet weight can give a slowly sinking effect of a dying baitfish. Similar to a fluke, this can be worked sporadically with a quick jerk of the rod tip, causing the tube to dart erratically like forage trying to evade capture in its final throes of life. If the fall rate is too slow for the current you are in, add a split shot sinker to the belly of the hook. Adjust the weight forward or back to change how the bait falls. Experimentation is key to this presentation.

The "Stupid Tube" is another means of rigging a tube snagless, while still maintaining the characteristic death spiral fall of the open rig. It's too complicated to explain here, so simply search the internet for "stupid tube" and you'll find lots of tutorials on how to rig this way. It takes a bit of practice to get just right, but if you're not a fan of dealing with snags, this is a good alternative to open rigging. It doesn't look and feel exactly the same, but I'm not sure smallmouths are all that fussy.

The "E-Z Tube" is another weedless way to rig tubes. The E-Z Tube is an internal weighted system created by the Lindner brothers that allows the use of an EWG hook, similar to Texas rigging, but with the weight inserted inside the tube. The EWG hook point passes through a hole in the weight, before passing back out the side of the tube. Since Lindy E-Z Tube weights are difficult to come by, Mike Iaconelli popularized the use of bell sinkers for the same purpose, using the eye of the sinker to hold the weight in place. This is likely the most natural weedless system that allows for all the characteristics of open rigging, without the exposed hook.

Skirted Jigs

Presentation: *it crawls, it swims*

Most largemouth bass anglers will be familiar with the ½ oz skirted jig and trailer as being a staple in their tackle box, but when you downsize the presentation to ¼ oz or less, this can be a deadly combination for smallmouth as well.

The power of a finesse skirted jig is not unlike that of your basic jig head and trailer combination, representing something small and tantalizing to the smallmouth. However, what sets this presentation apart is the flowing undulation of the silicone skirt. Even in a gentle current, when that jig comes to rest on the bottom, the skirt is still in motion. When jigged rhythmically, that skirt will puff out, collapse, and puff out again, not unlike the profile of a swimming crayfish.

I typically tip my jig with a soft plastic trailer representing a crayfish, or use a pork chunk (or plastic alternative), or recently I've been making my own claws and twister tail silhouettes from strips of leather. I dress the jig up with anything that will bulk up the profile and add the look of appendages.

I work a skirted jig in all the same ways I work a tube, by dragging, hopping and snapping along the bottom, or swimming through the water column. The advantage of the skirted jig over the open rigging of a tube is that I will be more confident to throw the skirted jig into brush piles and laydowns, because of the weed guard.

There aren't a lot of options on the market for smaller, finesse sized skirted jigs, Strike King Bitsy Bug being the main one. Z-man is also getting into the game with the Crosseyez and the ShroomZ Micro Finesse Jig. I've recently started making my own by adding a weed guard and skirt to a basic 1/4 ball head jig, which is a very economical option considering the abuse these jigs are subjected to.

Hair Jigs

Presentation: *it swims, it crawls*

Hair jigs, like a bucktail jig, or a marabou jig, are underrated lures that are typically reserved for cold water conditions. However, I use them all year, because when I tie them myself, they are cost effective and less environmentally impactful than the many soft plastic alternatives.

Hair jigs come in all shapes and sizes for all different applications, from your basic bucktail or marabou (which comprises some hair tied to a jig head), to elaborate crayfish, minnow and fly patterns designed to mimic natural forage. Hair jigs keep their free-flowing action regardless of the water temperature, which makes them essential in colder water where soft plastics start to become more rigid.

I will fish a hair jig much the same way that I fish a skirted jig or a tube, with all manner of bottom presentations, but I find the most productive presentations are when I am swimming a hair jig just off the bottom. Sometimes I'll add a jig spinner (beetle spin) for a little added flair, but otherwise, a hair jig is the ultimate do-little bait.

Depending on the current I'm fishing, the weight I use will range from $1/8$ oz to $1/4$ oz jigs. The head shape will vary, but if I make them myself, they will typically be a simple ball head jig. I will sometimes add a weed guard, and depending on the application, I may tip the hook with a plastic, leather or pork rind chunk, or curly tail.

Swimbait & Grubs

Presentation: *it swims*

Arguably two of the most popular and productive lures ever used in smallmouth bass fishing are the paddle tail swimbait and its forerunner, the curly tail grub. I lump them together in one category, since the applications of each are nearly indistinguishable for me. Wherever I'd use a swimbait, I'd use a grub, and vice versa.

These two presentations should mimic small, minnow sized baitfish. The paddle tail will offer a little more kick and wobble than the grub, but otherwise, their characteristics are very similar; a body and a tail that imparts action on the lure as it swims through the water column.

When I am targeting smallmouth that are 18 inches and up, I will use either a 3.5 to 4 inch paddle tail, or I will use a 5 inch grub. Colors will typically be some variation of all white or amber (grubs are usually a single color), or a white belly and brown, gray or blue back.

Both swimbaits and grubs are commonly used as trailers for all manner of skirted jigs, A-rigs, chatterbaits, and spinnerbaits, to add a little flair and impart some additional action. However, they are equally effective on their own, rigged on a jig head, or weighted EWG hook.

You can work a grub or swimbait like you would any soft plastic, but I feel their true power lies in swimming through the water column, just above the bottom, or swimming up and down through various depths with some stop-and-go reeling. Adding a pause or a twitch during your retrieve can often trigger a strike from any smallmouth who was just having a look.

Crankbaits

Presentation: *it swims*

I have a love/hate relationship with crankbaits in rivers. I don't use crankbaits all that often, so I don't catch a lot of smallmouths on them, but when I do, they are big, and they hit unbelievably hard. Crankbaits are loud (even without a rattle), and create a lot of commotion, drawing reaction bites from smallies that cross its path.

Crankbaits in rivers can be difficult since you need to keep reeling them in fast in order to keep up with the current. There is also a lot that a crankbait (and all its treble hooks) can get hung up on. However, once you find the perfect run for a crankbait—bouncing it off rocks and digging into gravel—you'll be rewarded by hooking up with only the meanest, most aggressive smallies.

In faster currents there isn't a lot of opportunity to vary the retrieve, but when you can, and when the current allows, you should try to add the odd burn and pause. Often, bumping rocks on the riverbed offers enough variety as this will cause the crankbait to deflect in different directions, giving the appearance of a baitfish changing course.

The selection of crankbaits at your local tackle shop will be nearly endless, but some mainstays for smallmouth bass fishing are Cotton Cordell's Big O in a craw pattern, the Rebel Craw (and Rebel Wee Craw), Rapala's DT6 in a craw or shad pattern, and Berkley's Digger in a craw or shad pattern.

Something to consider when using crankbaits in the river is the abuse they endure and the risk of losing them. If your crankbait isn't grinding the bottom or getting hung up, it's not catching fish. With all that bumping and grinding, your lure may not last, or may require regular tune-ups. Given that crankbaits are relatively expensive, you might spare your crankbaits from the torment of running through rivers.

Jerkbaits

Presentation: *it struggles, it swims*

Jerkbaits and smallmouths go together like fish and chips. There is something about a jerkbait that smallmouths find so irresistible, they cannot help themselves. You can see their curiosity as they chase a darting jerkbait from side to side, trying hard to get a better look, until one of them can't resist any more and finally commits.

Jerkbaits are one of the more versatile hard baits; they can be worked with erratic snaps of the rod with pauses in between, causing the bait to dart wildly back and forth, or they can be reeled with a steady retrieve like a crankbait. If reeled slowly, and you have the variety of jerkbait that floats, you can work it like a wake bait. This was one of the popular retrieves of the original Rapala Floating Minnow.

No matter how you work a jerkbait, the behavior and profile can mimic a baitfish in peak form, or a minnow in its last throes of life, and for that reason, the smallies cannot resist it. More than once I've hooked up with two and three bass at a time. Once you've got one interested, they all start to compete for the lure.

Mighty Smallmouth

It's only fitting that Rapala, the progenitor of the jerkbait, hold two or three of the top spots for the jerkbait category with behemoths like the X-Rap, Husky Jerk, Shadow Rap, Original Floater and others. Rapala continues to improve upon the minnow style jerkbait with new advances on appearance, action, and castability each year. Other contenders in the market are Yo-Zuri, Strike King, and Lucky Craft, but I've honestly never made it past the Rapala lineup to give an honest opinion.

Honorable mention goes to the soft plastic jerkbaits, which can range from a traditional stick bait (Senko) to a super fluke. These are also highly effective at attracting bass, but with a single texposed hook, you can miss some strikes aimed at maiming an already injured minnow presentation.

Spinnerbait

Presentation: *it swims*

Spinnerbaits are my number one go-to search bait on an unfamiliar stretch of river. They are useful in larger, slower pools, where I want to cover a lot of water in a short amount of time. I can run them along the bank, down a drop-off, I can run them high near the surface or bump them along the bottom and anywhere in between. Being remarkably weedless, I have confidence in throwing a spinnerbait into just about any cover without fear of it getting caught up.

I will vary my retrieve depending on how high or low in the water column I want to run the spinnerbait. In the early spring or late fall I may run it lower and slower, but more often than not I am burning a spinnerbait pretty fast. A lot of times, my lure is hammered the instant it hits the water, but if not, I will always add twitches and pauses in my retrieve to impart a little stutter and zing. Bites will come when the bait hits the water, or when the bait passes by some cover, or when I twitch and pause on the retrieve.

I will use ½ oz, white and chartreuse spinnerbaits with tandem willow blades, almost exclusively, when I am targeting smallmouth bass. I rarely add a plastic trailer unless I'm looking to add some lift while slow-rolling the bait. I find between the blades and the shimmy of the silicone skirt I don't need the added action a trailer brings. However, I do sometimes add additional silicone skirts to help bulk up the profile, or add some accenting colors.

Spinnerbaits are generally cost effective because they are durable, highly modifiable, and can be refreshed and maintained season after season with new blades and new skirts. The hook is stout enough to be repeatedly sharpened over many seasons. With that said though, I favor brands that hold up to the abuse, like Northland Tackle, Booyah, and Strike King.

Topwater

Presentation: *it floats*

If you were to ask 100 anglers their favorite way to catch smallmouth bass, 99 of them would tell you topwater lures are the most exciting, heart pounding way to get a bite. There is nothing like working a topwater across the surface of the river and having a trophy bronze back suddenly, and violently breach the water, hellbent on destroying your lure. Even when you are expecting a strike, nothing prepares you for that explosive sound and the eruption of water.

Of all the lures, topwater's have to be the most innovative with the greatest variety, both in purpose and in configuration. From lures that target specific areas, like weed edges and laydowns, to lures that cover open water. From slow and steady to a quick burn, there is a topwater for every application. Let's cover a few of the more popular styles of topwater lures for smallmouths.

Poppers

As a lure that is worked more slowly, poppers are best suited for targeted casts around structures you suspect might hold bass. Many poppers are capable of a walking action if worked just right, but they excel simply as a popping bait, breaking the surface of the water with the cupped mouth, providing that tantalizing spitting sound and action.

Many modern poppers are weighted so that they can be cast a long way, which is important if your popper also acts as a walking bait. Otherwise, I'm making very targeted casts, popping my way past a point of interest, burning it back in and making another targeted cast. For my retrieve, a simple rhythm of twitch-twitch-pause seems to do the trick. If you're fishing in faster current, maintain a constant popping action, like a frog or toad trying to swim to shore.

Some of the more famous poppers are the Rebel Pop-R and the Arbogast Hula Popper, but my favorite popper as of late is the Berkley Bullet Pop. The Bullet Pop has a great weight to size ratio and it floats tail-down, making it spit water with ease and walk with little effort.

Walking Baits

If you need to cover water a little more quickly, but still want a slower bait to keep in the strike zone a little longer, then a walking bait is a good choice. Smallies can't seem to resist that side to side, walk-the-dog action and will blow up on a walking bait multiple times until they're finally snagged.

You need relatively calm water to work a walking bait properly, and a slower current will help with your cadence. If the current is too fast, trying to pick up too much slack while trying to maintain a walking action can be exhausting. You can vary your retrieve speed, depending on the mood of the bass. Sometimes changing the speed mid retrieve will trigger a strike, or sometimes a well-placed pause will entice a smallmouth to hammer the lure clear out of the water.

Walking baits are typically on the larger side, but I prefer smaller ones, especially on more confined rivers. My favorite is the Heddon Super Spook Jr which is only 3 ½ inches long. Other notable brands are the Storm Arashi Top Walker, Strike King Sexy Dog Jr, and the Berkley J-Walker.

Prop Baits

Propeller baits or "prop" baits are generally lures that have some sort of propeller that, when pulled through the water, will cause disturbance on the surface. Some of the more well known are the Whopper Plopper and the Torpedo.

The proper retrieve for prop baits will depend on the lure. Whopper Ploppers, Choppos, and TopRaiders are all intended to be fished fairly fast and steady to cover a lot of water. I've also had success in popping, twitching and jerking them as well. A Devil's Horse or Torpedo, on the other hand, is for targeted casts, meant to be worked more slowly, like a popper.

The River2Sea Whopper Plopper 75 and 90 are both solid performers, but they are wildly expensive. I opt for the Berkley Choppo 75 and 90 as they are considerably cheaper and perform equally well. For the twitch and pop style prop baits, the Heddon Tiny Torpedo can't be beat. The Rapala Skitter Pop and the original Smithwick Devil's Horse are also popular alternatives with more of a minnow profile.

One tip I can offer on most top waters, but on prop baits especially, is to use a fairly heavy test monofilament leader. Monofilament line floats, and the added stiffness will keep your line projected away from the lure and avoid getting tangled in the propellers.

Wakebaits

Wakebaits look a lot like crankbaits, and some models would easily be mistaken for one. But like many classes of lures, they come in many shapes and sizes, all having the common behavior of swimming across the surface realistically, causing an undulating wake.

The bill on the front of a wake bait is nearly straight up and down, pushing water and causing the bait to wobble and roll from side to side. In jointed wakebaits, this roll causes the lure to pivot back and forth slightly, giving the appearance of a swimming mouse or rat. If you've ever seen Matt Nelson (NDYakAngler) on YouTube, you may be familiar with the Spro Rat and just how realistic a presentation it is.

Wakebaits are fairly easy to use, just cast and reel back with a fairly slow retrieve. There is no need for twitches or pauses, the wobble and roll is enough to trigger a strike.

There are too many wakebait makes and configurations to list, but some go-to examples are the Spro Rat, Berkeley Wakebull, Arbogast Jitterbug, and the Yo-Zuri 3DR Wakebait.

Summary

There are so many lure categories and combinations to choose from, they can't all be covered here. Hopefully, this gives you an idea of where to start. Any time I go out fishing, I take a single 3600 series plano box with me containing 4 to 6 lures and some soft plastics. Most of the summer my tackle bag contains a Berkley Choppo, a Heddon Super Spook Jr, a Northland Tackle Spinnerbait, some Strike King Bitsybug jigs, some ball head jigs and some tubes, grubs and paddle tail swimbaits.

One area I covered little, beyond tubes, paddle tails and grubs, was the vast array of soft plastic baits and the myriad of ways to rig them. One of the most exciting aspects of fishing is the endless innovation that goes into it. Anglers are always coming up with new ways to present old lures. Honorable mention goes to the drop shot and its many variations (power shot, tube shot, Ned shot and others), the free rig, Tokyo rig, jika rig, Carolina rig, Texas rig, the mojo rig, whacky rig, neko rig... the list goes on forever. All it takes to come up with something new is some inspiration, innovation and a few bits of hardware.

And of course, a huge shout-out goes to the Ned rig. There are some setups that catch an insane amount of smallmouth bass, big and small, and the Ned rig is one of them. But I'm not after numbers of fish, I'm chasing trophy bass, 18 inches or bigger. A tube and a Ned rig are essentially the same presentation and both catch insane numbers of smallies. However, 95% of the Ned rig catches will be 14 inches or less, while 95% of the tube catches will be 16 or bigger. When you're after big fish, throw bigger baits.

A Practical Approach

As I collected my thoughts, experiences and research for this book, I found defining the theory for what I did naturally in practice was somewhat difficult. By the time I had completed the previous chapters, I was questioning whether everything that I had surmised, or that simply felt natural to me, actually translated well into teachings that could help others on the water.

Thankfully, by the time I had finished all the preceding text, fishing season was upon me, and I put all my theory to the test by applying everything I'd written to entirely new sections of river as yet unexplored by me. The aim was to see if my gut was right about seasons, features, active bass, and lures. I wanted to see if my overall knowledge could produce trophy bass anywhere I felt the conditions were conducive to it.

The tales that follow recount a fishing season's worth of exploration on skinny water to put my knowledge to the test. I'll break down how I chose the locations, what I looked for and how I broke down the water in each case. I'm thrilled that the practical experience was every bit as reliable as the theory laid out. I'm even more happy that I learned more along the way.

Adapting to Change over Time

I have a favorite spot on the Grand River that is a 12 minute drive from my house, followed by a 5 minute paddle downstream. I've fished this hole for years, so I know all its features, its holes, sandbars, boulders, weed lines and such. It's a fairly large section of river that covers 27,000 square meters, but I'm familiar with its structure from riffle to glide.

In all the seasons I've fished this spot there had never been a significant drought until 2022. When I had revisited this spot for the first time late in the summer of that year, I was shocked to find that a full season of low flows had drastically changed the bottom composition and habitat. What didn't surprise me was the lack of bass in all the usual haunts.

In 2022 after a dry summer, and low flows, lighter sediment had continued to build until the bottom composition in some of my favorite pockets was silted over. Usually higher flows ensure this sediment is washed out regularly. The buildup this year had allowed large matts of grass to take hold and had also brought in carp by the dozens. There were no bass to be found in the usual spots.

I wasn't ready to give up on my favorite fishing hole just yet. I drifted down to the glide, where the flow picked up and more rocks were sure to be exposed. Sure enough, I found the rocks, and I found some bass, but not the size I was used to. Given the hot, dry summer, I knew the water was pretty warm this year, and the oxygen would be in short supply. I was either going to find them near the weeds, or in the run, as close to the riffle as they could hold.

The weed lines produced a few fish, but it was up near the riffle, and strong current, that I finally found both numbers and size of fish that I was after. I've never had much luck fishing the run in this fishing spot. There's a strong current here, and given the abundant places to hold in typical years, fighting this current has never been a necessity for these fish. It was only when the conditions were right that the bass could find no other logical location to hold.

Over the course of two outings at this spot, I focused on the run and found dozens of 16 inch bass, and pulled out an 18 inch, a 20 inch and a 21.25 inch bass. Each one was lighter than their lengths would typically suggest, which was expected given the energy output and comparatively low forage base in the higher current.

Smallmouth bass are survivors. As humans we like simple, repeatable, reliable patterns but sometimes mother nature throws a curveball to both the bass and anglers. Many fishers might consider the hole to be "fished out" when they can't find bass in what was once a plentiful fishery. The observant and ever-thinking angler will try to understand what's changed from the season before and use their knowledge of bass behavior to find where they've moved to.

Catching Big Bass on Small Water

Strong currents have kept this 20-inch bass lean.

Finding Spots On Satellite Maps

On a warm sunny day in August I explored an abandoned bridge area that showed promise on Google Maps. From the satellite view I could see well-worn trails that lead to what appeared to be a deep pool, and what was sure to be a community fishing hole.

This area wasn't the object of my investigation, however. I was more interested in the compact nature of the riffle-run-pool-glide sequence that was also clear on satellite view. A few hundred meters up or downstream showed what had the potential to be deceptively deep pockets in what was otherwise very skinny water.

Upon arrival I made a quick exploration of what was, in fact, a community hole. It was worth looking into on a future visit, but I was more interested in working upstream this time around. I began the journey on foot, waders on, up river across rocks that were the size of tennis balls. This made the trek cumbersome, putting an enormous strain on my back and knees, and the first 200 meters was a long, uninhabitable riffle. The first pool was a bust; very shallow with long patches of grass. I pulled out a few yearling bass, but that was all this shallow water was going to support.

It wasn't until I reached the top of the second riffle, nearly 400 meters upstream, that I could see the darker water of a deeper pool take shape. I started to make more targeted casts at what looked like high percentage areas; a current break, ripple in the water, an undercut bank...

And then I saw it—the sharp outside corner at the tail of a longer bend creating a small, slow eddy. There was a fallen tree at the back of the eddy, accentuating the circular current, and a series of large boulders at the start, barely visible below the water's surface. This small but magical location will hold at least one giant smallmouth.

I had one, maybe two casts into the little pocket before my presence was known and my chances were gone. I chose a line that would pull my topwater lure downstream, and just overhead the leeward side of those boulders I spotted.

The first cast was wide, falling to the backside of the eddy. I knew this errant cast would have little impact as I was certain nothing was back there to be spooked. My next cast had to be spot on, and it was. Sailing towards the bank, just before the start of the eddy, my lure landed with a gentle plop on the water's surface. I began my retrieve.

I typically add strategic pauses to my floating topwater retrieves, but in this case the distance I was reeling was too short, and I wanted to get across the backend of the boulders before drifting out of position. I reeled from the bank to the boulders in one, smooth retrieve. As soon as the lure reached the boulder, the water erupted and my bait was sucked under the surface.

I waited a beat, then swept the rod tip to seat the hook points firmly, but gently enough not to tear the fish's mouth parts. I could tell by the resistance on the end of my line that this was a solid bass. Indeed, after a protracted fight in the rocks, I raised a 19.5 inch spotted beauty from the river.

Mighty Smallmouth

Exploring can be rewarding when you know what to look for

Overlooked Community Holes

I spend a lot of time on satellite view (Google Maps, Google Earth) looking for promising areas of the river. I look for riffles which are fairly visible on most satellite imagery. Then I observe the pool that follows to see if it looks deep enough, has the telltale signs of slower flow rate, or has any interesting structure in the water or on the bank.

I also look to see how accessible the area is. If the potential hole is near residential neighborhoods, has trail access, is near a bridge or road, or has a boat launch nearby, I generally assume that the fish there are fairly pressured. Knowing that most weekend anglers won't get in the water to wade, I look for the spot-on-the-spot that might be less accessible.

That was the case in early August, 2022 when I fished a spot near a bridge, and a public park, and had a regular stream of kayakers and rafters drifting through. The park was a well-known destination for dog walkers, paddlers, and picnickers from miles around. All summer long this park serves as a popular launch and pickup point for many rafting outfits eager to cool their patrons in the summer flows.

On satellite view I could see the bridge spanning over the river as it bifurcated around a couple of islands. Just before the bridge were the riffles that fed the north and south channel, and just after the bridge were two slack-water pools of nearly equal length. However, the north channel was wider, and the riffle that fed it looked more constricted and turbulent. This was the pool that would have depth and exposed aggregate. With the park and canoe launch on the south bank, and sizable over-

Mighty Smallmouth

grown islands separating the north and south channels, I knew the north channel pool would be harder to access for the average weekend fisher. I knew the pressure there would be significantly less.

I waded my way across the river, downstream of where the two channels merge, and made my way to the north bank of the trailing island. From there I worked my way slowly upstream towards the bridge and the leading island. Having never explored this section of river, I had no way of knowing how deep the water might get on this section, but surmising it was the tail end of the glide from the pool ahead, I suspected the water would be shallow enough to wade.

I finally reached the tail end of the pool just ahead of the glide. The current was swift on the surface, but I could just make out the telltale signs of current seams and breaks that gave away the position of changes in the bottom contours. There was a long submerged point coming out from the island and it was creating a slight back current with a pronounced seam dividing the two flows. I took one cast with a skirted jig and crawfish trailer just to get a sense of the bottom composition. Sure enough, it was strewn with softball sized rounded rocks. This was going to be the spot-on-a-spot.

On the very next cast, right on the edge of the current seam, I felt the familiar tick of a bass picking up my bait. I monitored my line to watch for lateral movement, but there wasn't any. Either my lure was dropped, or the fish was big enough to rule that part of the river. I gently raised my rod until I could feel tension, and that's when I felt the slight tug back. With a mighty swing I set the weedless, single-hook jig, sending the heavy fish into a frenzy.

With a few great leaps and a mad dash downstream, I was almost certain I would lose whatever was on my line. The fish's only mistake was to make a run behind me into the slack water of the eddy created by the point. This allowed me the opportunity to reel in some slack and gain some ground on the thrashing beast. When all was said and done, I landed a 19 inch, battle-worn brown spotted smallmouth.

I caught another 3 great specimens in the course of the next hour.

I was richly rewarded for my exploration that day, and venturing where so few are willing to go. It's always worthwhile checking out community holes, but looking for angles, opportunities or presentations that others may not have tried. Look for harder-to-access areas that the typical weekend angler won't attempt.Often a community spot will be restricted to one bank, so try fishing the other side. Here, I had to traverse one channel and make my way upstream in the opposite channel. It wasn't an easy trip, but worth going the extra distance for some great fishing.

Mighty Smallmouth

It pays to go the extra mile to find less-pressured fish.

New Sructure, Changing Habitat

One of my favorite local rivers is a small, slow flowing mature system that lazily meanders through farmland and countryside. What makes the Nith such an interesting river to fish is that it reinvents itself every year. With no flood control the Nith becomes a raging torrent every spring, carving steep bluffs through the sandy river basin. The Nith will change course by several feet over the course of a year as banks erode, trees are toppled over.

One spot that I frequented often was suddenly transformed in 2022. Previously, the predominant feature was a large tree-fall, its trunk facing downstream and root ball facing upstream. Over many years, the tree sank further and further into the depths as the river's current eroded the soft substrate beneath it. The hole created by current washing around the tree was nearing 7 feet deep and held many great fish.

In 2022, the entire tree had been washed away. All that remained was a deep, silt filled pool, edged by a small, unassuming tree stump and root ball that had recently washed in. The stump had come to settle on the edge of the pool, with one side sitting in a foot of water while the other side teetered the edge of a steep bank plunging into the watery depths of the hole left by the previous season's fallen tree.

I cast my Berkley Choppo past the stump, downstream, to the deeper side of the stump. By reeling upstream, I was hoping to keep the lure in the strike zone longer, while maintaining optimum chop. I couldn't have timed it more perfectly if I tried. The instant my lure was alongside the stump, the water's surface broke in an angry flurry of water.

I waited a beat, then swept my rod to the side to ensure a solid hook set. The fish felt heavy, sure to be a trophy bass. She leapt from the water, confirming my suspicions of her size. Upon landing she dove away from the stump and into the depths of the once tree-filled hole. I was not sure what was down there so I quickly tried to wrestle her back towards the surface. I'd rather have risked losing her from a head shaking leap out of the water than break her off on some unknown submerged structure.

I kept her from the hole, and the stump she was hiding under, and finally landed her after a few close encounters between her and my wader-clad legs. Once I had her unhooked and lifted from the water, I gazed upon her dark, defined bars and spots. She measured just under 19 inches.

Rivers are ever changing and bass are continually adapting to that change. If you are keenly aware of this change, you can use it to your advantage. Observe how the structure changes, what new foreign objects might have washed in or out, how banks have eroded, and how the bottom composition has changed. An area that was conducive to holding bass last season may no longer be appealing this season. The opposite is also true, look for new fish-holding opportunities in the river, new laydowns, or obstructions that have the potential to create deeper holes and pockets over time.

Catching Big Bass on Small Water

A newly washed in stump provided a refuge for this bass

Oasis in the Desert

A short drive from my house is a small plot of crown land that backs on to a narrow stretch of river. It is the perfect spot to take my dog swimming. The stretch we typically wade is slow and skinny with several deeper pools for her to swim bank to bank to cool off. We usually make a pretty lazy afternoon of it, but I'll bring my rod for something to do.

On a hot, sunny day in mid-August, my dog came to my home office around noon, bugging me to go swimming. So off we went to the river to cool off. I found the water as refreshing as she did so I was in no rush to leave after we walked our usual length of river. I kept wading further downstream, into waters I'd never been to. I'd scoped these waters out on satellite view, and figured it wasn't worth the extra miles. I could tell it was wide, shallow, and probably silty. It seemed relatively featureless as well, with no visible deviation in depth or visible rock piles.

My initial suspicions were mostly confirmed, this stretch was in fact wide and featureless. However, it was a foot or so deeper than I had suspected, and instead of being silty, the riverbed consisted of coarse sand, and the water was crystal clear. There were some sparse patches of grass here and there, and a recent laydown washed out in the very middle of this expansive flat. I figured if there was anything in this stretch, on this blazingly hot, clear sky afternoon, it would be around that tree.

I cast to that tree from every angle and couldn't pick up a bite. I figured it was time to move on from this general area and accept that nothing was here. Before starting out, I made one last cast, but this time in the direction I was headed.

One habit of mine when I'm river wading is to cast ahead, in the direction I'm due to walk in. It's more of a superstition than a tactic, but I figure if there were any fish in my path, I'd want to know about them before walking through and spooking them. Today was no different.

I made a long bomb cast downstream into the middle of nowhere, and started burning my top water bait across the surface. This had to be the clearest, sparsest, sunniest, gin-clear patch of water, and I had no expectations beyond clearing the path in front of me. Out of nowhere, an angry beast of a bass just hammers my lure.

With no obstructions between her and I, the fight was little more than a tug of war between us. I can't recall a fight on the river that was in such crystal-clear water. The water was so clear I could see her eyes move as she tracked my location in proximity to the end of the line she was fighting against.

After measuring her at 18 inches, I released her and watched as she swam back to the same relative area I caught her. Out of curiosity I followed her path to see what she could hold on in that wide, vast expanse. When I approached where I thought she ought to have been, I saw her dart out from behind the only boulder in the whole area. In this vast, wide, flat expanse of coarse sand, this smallmouth found the one boulder to set up on.

Mighty Smallmouth

A completely unexpected catch, always keep an open mind

Worth the Wade

For a couple of years I had a location in mind that I had scoped on satellite imagery; a long, slow looking pool, immediately after a tight, wide bend that looked like a remarkably shallow riffle. I knew by key features it would not be easy to get to. I could have easily paddled there, but pulling out where I put in might have been a significant effort and I had yet to coordinate a day float with a pickup downstream.

I had scoped further upstream in previous years, and found the current in the section moved quite fast. I knew that heading downstream on foot would be tough unless the conditions were right. That was the case in 2022 with prolonged dry spells and record low flows. I knew if I was going to wade down river to this location, this would be the year for it.

Around the same time, a fishing buddy and I were exchanging spots we've tried in the river. I mentioned this bend and long pool that I was looking to explore, and he immediately recognized the location. He had fished there before, and had tips where he's found them in the past. He had stressed the run as being the high percentage area, but gave up few other details.

On a comfortable evening in mid-August, I slipped on the old waders and made my way downstream from a public canoe launch. The water ran fairly clear, so I didn't have too much trouble picking my way through the shallow, yet quick current. When I hit the first part of the bend, I wasn't able to see the bottom immediately ahead of me, and given the water had taken a deep blue hue, I suspected I was about to step into a scour hole. I considered walking through it, but one or two steps in, I knew it was going to get too deep for comfort, so I backed my way out, and moved closer to the inside of the river.

I was in a fairly fast flowing section with the bend in the river causing the current to pick up speed as it rounded the corner. I had to be very sure-footed on this outside section, especially with a hole of unknown depth behind me. The potential of that scour hole had me curious. I wanted to know how deep it was, and could it possibly hold fish with such a strong current around it? For curiosity's sake, I tossed my skirted jig towards the upstream edge of the hole, and let the current take my lure into its blue depths.

I didn't get the chance to gauge its depths. Before my lure could hit bottom, a heavy brute of a smallmouth picked up my jig and made for the outside bank. I fought the fish for a quick stint until it swung into the swift flow in the middle of the riffle. At that point, the current, and the fighting fish, were far too strong to reel in. I attempted to move out of the strong flow, but I wasn't as sure on my feet as I would have liked. In a matter of moments, that smallie had pulled off, but not before getting a good sense of its size. It could have been anywhere from 18 to 20 inches, but a life in the current had left it on the leaner side, from what I could tell.

I carried on downstream and made my way past the riffle and started exploring the run, but from the relative comfort of the inside bend within calmer water. This was the high percentage area my friend had recommended I focus on. I caught several smaller specimens but any fish of substance was eluding me. I only had an hour of sunlight to explore the spot, so I continued my way down from the run to explore the lengths of the pool.

The water was still clear enough for me to make out structures and boulders to cast at. By this point I was working a top water lure to cover water quickly. I was excited by the attention I was getting with missed blowups, a sign there was a healthy population of eager bass in the section of river.

Towards the back of the pool, on the leeward side of a point, stood a small stand of trees. With a current break, and trees for shade and cover, I knew this would be a high percentage spot. I assessed the area to determine what cast would be most advantageous. Typically, you get one chance with a topwater, and I wanted to make sure I gave myself the opportunity for the highest percentage placement of my bait.

The river was too wide at this point for me to cast to the far bank, so I carefully felt my way through the hip-deep water. I gave one cast just downstream of the first tree, landing about 6 inches from the bank. I reeled back upstream at a slight angle, letting the current carry the lure downstream. The overall effect was a course that was almost perpendicular to the bank, and keeping the lure as close to the pocket as I could manage.

The topwater bait ran a line right across the river, uninterrupted until it had come about 6 feet towards me from the opposite shore. That's when the water exploded with a mighty slap. I waited a beat and gave a steady sideways sweep of the rod and knew immediately that I was hooked up with a sizable smallmouth bass. With the current being a little more lax, the fish leaped a few times, before bearing down and diving for the rocks.

I was still mid-river during the fight and carefully tried to edge my way back to shallower water. Once the water was thigh-deep, the brute made a mad dash for wader-clad legs. I was worried she'd trip me up, or get a hook stuck in my waders. I worked her back through my legs, and with a little more effort, I grabbed her by the lip and raised her from the water. She was a beautiful, tiger-striped, light colored specimen without a single flaw or blemish on her.

With daylight running short, I had to take my leave of this section of river and make my way to an access point downstream, but not without noting the other fishing opportunities that might be fruitful on future visits. Upon a post-expedition wrap up with my fishing buddy, he admitted that where I caught the big girl was where he focuses his attention when looking for the big ones. He had withheld the information to see if I'd find them there myself.

I returned to the same location a few more times in the season, both on foot and in a kayak, and learned more about its overall structure. The area that produced, not only had trees for shade, as well as an eddy for a current break, but also has a distinct ledge for fish to relate to. It's always nice to know your own study of a location matches that of another angler.

Two anglers finding the spot-on-a-spot can't be luck.

Keep an Open Mind

It always seems my fishing opportunities don't line up with others in my fishing community, so when I get the chance to fish with others, I take it. I find I learn a lot from others, watching their cadence, their patterns and their approach to breaking down a section of river, whether their tactics work.

On one such occasion I was invited to explore a location that my friend Cam had been frequenting with great success. I had passed through this location once before on a paddling trip. I could see it had potential, but I had since overlooked this spot when viewed on satellite. As seen from above it lacked some of the telltale signs of fish holding structure and was somewhat straight and featureless. What I could see, however, was riffles. Where there are riffles, there are pools.

Had it not been for the invite from Cam, this spot might have remained unchecked on my list for years to come. Having the chance to go with a friend was a perfect opportunity to learn my way in and out. I was also recovering from a bad leg injury, so having someone to look out for me was a bonus.

Upon arrival, early one weekday morning, we made our way down a community trail to a well-used river access point. From there we picked our way along the bank, heading downstream for 300 meters. The section we were bypassing was swift and shallow and not terribly productive looking. In fact, during my paddle through here years prior, the bottom composition was mostly shale and only inches deep for long stretches.

We finally arrived at what I could only describe as the long tail of a run, after what seemed like a 300 meter long riffle. If you weren't familiar with the river sequences, you'd almost miss that we had transitioned into the run by this point. The water was still fairly fast, and with these low, late summer flows, it was more turbulent than it would be earlier in the season.

I watched Cam as he cast directly across the current and dragged back a bottom presentation perpendicular to the bank. He caught several decent fish this way, but we were looking for tanks. I worked my way slightly downstream and more into the current. Cam's presentation showed promise, but I wondered if only the smaller, most agile fish were going to put up a chase as a lure passed by their nose.

I positioned myself about 10 feet towards the middle of the river and cast upstream, virtually the same presentation as his, a skirted jig with a craw trailer. The hope was to work my lure downstream, keeping my presentation in front of any unsuspecting bass who are already nose-up into the current. This would allow my lure to stay in the strike zone longer. The tactic paid off. Within three casts of me picking off visible current breaks, I felt the undeniable "thonk" of a big bronze back aggressively snatching a craw out of the rocks.

As quickly as I'd set the hook, I felt the line get slack immediately. I was sure I had missed the strike, but noticed my line moving in an unnatural direction downstream and away from me. I quickly reeled up as much slack as I could and set the hook again. She was still on!

Mighty Smallmouth

It was a constant struggle for me trying to reel up slack as she raced towards me, and towards Cam's line. That's when things got complicated, as our lines had become crossed in the water. He was on the bank while I was in the river in a swift current and large rocks to navigate through. We carefully worked our way towards each other to get the mess sorted out while the smallmouth continued to fight on the other end.

My injured leg was making this more difficult and treacherous, and one missed step over a large rock had me falling into the river. I maintained control over the smallmouth while Cam helped me to my feet. We finally got ourselves untangled, giving me the opportunity to lift a thick, 18 inch trophy bass from the swift water.

Unfortunately, I couldn't stay for more exploration as my work day was starting shortly after that catch, but I was thankful to Cam for opening my eyes to an opportunity that would have otherwise remained overlooked. It just shows that all the research done over maps doesn't compare to exploration on foot or in a boat. In subsequent visits, both on foot and by kayak, I'd scoped out the entire pool, from run to glide, and it never failed to produce.

Catching Big Bass on Small Water

It was a bit of a circus to land this fish.

The Textbook Play

Frequently in 2022 when I explored new locations, I did not know what I was in for. There were times I'd arrive ready to wade, but the immediate access was too deep or too muddy to wade safely. I got into trouble the odd time, getting caught in water that was too fast or too deep, or the bottom would turn to silt and I'd sink up to my knees. These were the locations I'd go back to with a kayak at a later date.

Then there were the occasions where everything would turn out like a textbook play. Such was the case on a lunch time swim with my dog in early September. I knew of a decent canoe launch 20 minutes from my house and figured with the low water levels we'd been having, I'd probably be safe to attempt a wade there and give my dog the chance to cool off. I had scoped this location from a bridge a few years back as a potential put-in for my kayak, but we'd never explored this location from the water's edge.

As I had suspected, the dry summer made this access point more than doable for my dog and I. We slipped into the water and made our way upstream where I knew I'd find a steep gravel bluff wall at a bend in the river. I'd seen this feature in my research, clearly visible from satellite view, and was eager to see if there would be a deep cut river bottom, easily washed away with the current.

My dog and I trekked through 500 meters of a long, shallow riffle. There was the odd scour pool and washout, but nothing worthy of holding fish in these low flows. We continued upstream until we hit the top of the riffle, which acted as more of an impoundment. This created the effect of the pool remaining deep and slow almost right up to the riffle, with barely evidence of a glide.

The later part of the glide seemed a touch stagnant in the beating sun, but a couple of fallen brush piles held several smaller smallmouths. This gave me hope this bend would produce. I slogged my way around this narrow bend, able to cast from the shallow, inside bend, to the far bank. I was trying to get a sense of the bottom composition with a skirted jig, with a Jackall Cover Craw threaded on. It seemed fairly sandy and featureless, but was relatively deep, with a gradual slope towards the shallows where I was standing. This wasn't a surprise given the loose, sandy composition of the bluff wall on that side of the river.

I knew that hard structure would be the key to this section of river, and that depth alone wouldn't make for a comfortable holding place for any sizable smallmouth. I cast across the narrow water towards cuts in the bank, or washout points made by debris washing down the bluff. However, these current breaks were bathed in the full heat of the midday sun and weren't giving up any bites.

As I made my way upstream I was eager to cast towards a stand of trees that was soon to line the river's edge. The first tree in line was the only tree to overhang the waters edge enough to cast a shadow over the water, and I knew this would be the highest percentage spot on this whole stretch of river at this time of day. I didn't want to blow the spot with a fouled cast, so I waited until I was absolutely sure I could hit the exact upstream edge of the shaded water.

The area I was targeting was small, and I knew I'd only have one shot. I made the cast, hitting the water just inside of the shade line. I waited for the lure to hit bottom, paying out line as it dropped. Before the lure could touchdown, I felt the unmistakable, and sizable tap of a fairly aggressive bite. Before I could set the hook, I felt a weight on the line, and a headshake. I was worried she might have spit the hook at this point. Wasting no more time, I set the hook hard, and there was no give. It was as though I had set the hook into a tree, but the tree pulled back. That's when I knew I had something special on the end of the line.

The bass effortlessly traced a line up and down the river, pulling drag as she went. I fought to keep her contained within a short run to prevent her from hanging up in any unseen submerged laydowns. I wasn't able to draw her towards me, so I had to wade towards her while picking up line in my reel.

After several minutes I could see her broadside as I reeled her in closer to me. She had an unmistakable girth, and paddle-shaped tail of a true river giant. With a few more last bursts of fight, I got a hold of her and laid hands on a 20-inch beast. She was only the second fish over 4 pounds for me that season.

There is something so rewarding when I can research a location, and within an hour of leaving the house, have all my understanding and knowledge of river bass translate into a trophy smallmouth on the end of my line.

Catching Big Bass on Small Water

Sometimes you just know where they'll be.

Summary

In 2022 I explored new locations with nearly every outing. I had made a point of researching and fishing new water to validate what I understood of finding mighty smallmouth in rivers and creeks. Of the 20 or more new locations I fished, every one of them produced excellent fishing, and fifteen of them produced trophy smallmouth in my first outing there.

Having the awareness of time of day, fishable features, and signs of activity, allowed me to target oxygen rich riffles on a hot day, or a lone rock on a sun-bleached flat, a hard to reach pool with less pressure, or shoreline trees casting comfortable shade.

In any situation I could translate my understanding of rivers, and of bass behavior, into new fishing opportunities. In every situation I could get on great fish, and in many situations I could get on trophy smallmouths.

The Final Chapter

I've been wanting to write this book for years and I'm glad I've had the chance to get all my thoughts out of my head and into yours. Fishing for truly giant smallmouth bass is one part art, one part science, a lot of preference, and even more experience. Trial and error are the best teachers, and observation is the best textbook.

For general fishing, there are countless websites, books, and YouTube channels. For smallmouth bass there is significantly less material to draw from. For resources dedicated to fishing for big smallmouth on small rivers and streams, there isn't much at all, and even less that is still in print. That was my main reason for writing this book, to offer an insightful dive into this niche topic.

Finding and catching trophy smallmouth bass on small rivers can be daunting, but I hope you are now armed with the knowledge and tools to make your outings more fruitful. You don't need expensive gear, and a bottomless tackle box of lures to catch smallmouth. You don't need a fancy boat and high-tech electronics to find them. You just need an understanding of smallmouth habitat within a river, seasonal habits, and an ability to see and understand the conditions that can promote activity within a bass population.

For me, the best part of dialing in river smallies is the intimate connection gained with nature. I've had so many encounters with wildlife that I would have never experienced had it not been for spending time on the river, trying to unlock the secrets of the smallmouth bass, the secrets of the river. I've come within meters of deer who have become so accustomed to my presence that they hardly flinch when I paddle around the corner. I've had a huge old beaver swim through my legs as she looked to end a faceoff with my dog. I've had more than a few mink swim up to the kayak to check me out, and one foggy morning as I approached a rock, I had a mink clearly trying to decide whether it should hop in the boat with me or swim away.

To be a better smallmouth angler, you need time on the water. No amount of reading or watching YouTube can replace the practical experience of time spent in a river. Learn how your rivers work, how they change and what makes some areas hospitable, and others not. Then explore other rivers to see if the knowledge you've gained applies to other river systems. Observe everything from time of day, time of year, bottom composition, current, structure below and above the water's surface. Watch for birds, and watch for forage. Travel light, simplify your lure selection, and venture into new water often. Be a student of nature.

I hope you enjoyed Mighty Smallmouth: Catching Big Bass on Small Water, and I hope it helps you learn and explore your local waterways, and teaches you a thing or two about targeting bigger smallmouth bass. That's the best part about fishing; there is always something to learn, some innovation to try, some new personal best to achieve.

Tight lines!

Mighty Smallmouth

Acknowledgments

To the content creators who spend countless hours of their lives to share their knowledge with us. Be it books, video, podcasts or magazines, I've learned so much from the likes of Jeff Little, Matt Nelson, Benjamin Nowak, Collin Lamkin, Adam Leppert, Gord Pyser, Peter Bowman, Angelo Viola, Bob Izumi, Ashley Rae, Tony Bean, Jim Root, Mark Zona, Josh Chrenko, Chris Vaughan, and so many others whose content I've consumed, learned from, and shared over the years.

In my early years as an angler, fishing was an activity I did with my closest friends. I want to thank Bentley, my oldest childhood friend, for the many adventures (and misadventures) we took on our local waterways. From as close as Laurel Creek, and Grand River, to "far away" Bronte Creek (is there a bee in my hair?) and Lake Huron.

I want to thank "the boys", Chris, Nick and Harold, who have gathered annually in remote northern locations for weekends of outdoor immersion. Whether it's rolling quads in mud puddles, shooting rapids in our kayaks, or catching the world's smallest fish, there is never a dull moment when we are together. Adventure, exploration and friendship keeps us young.

It's hard to put into words what social media has done for fishing. It's certainly made it more accessible. But social media has also connected so many of us in ways that wouldn't have been possible in the past. I've fished with more fishing friends in the last couple years than I had my whole life. A big thanks to the kindness and generosity of new friends like Rob, Cam, Lucas, Matt, Amy, Ashley, Stephen, Michael, Paul, Shaun, Peter, John and so many more. We all love to share our knowledge and passion for fishing and I am truly lucky to have fished, learned, and shared with each of you.

I don't know if my son inherited from me, a passion for the outdoors, or a sickness. You were my constant outdoor companion growing up, from walks in the woods, to hiking near the river, and more fishing than is healthy for most humans. Thank you for continuing to talk about fishing, hunting, outdoors and general DIY hobbies from tackle crafting to bow making. You are more than a son; you are a best friend. I am only sorry that your fiance has to endure the same obsession with you as my wife endures from me.

To my wife and daughters who accept me for who I am. I will gladly hike seven hours in the woods without complaint but struggle to manage thirty minutes in a mall without excruciating back pain. I can't explain it. It's one of life's greatest mysteries. Our many years of camping and outdoor adventures will be cherished memories forever. Without your daily support I wouldn't be able to pursue the passions that I do.

And to my parents, who instilled in me a passion for the outdoors. Whether it was hiking along the cliffs of the Grand River, or camping in the northern reaches of the Bruce Peninsula, you always allowed me to be outdoors with no limits. You nurtured an appreciation of the natural world in me I've since passed on to my family.

www.ingramcontent.com/pod-product-compliance
Lightning Source LLC
Chambersburg PA
CBHW071457080526
44587CB00014B/2135